A BOY WITH DREAMS

JOURNEY IN SEARCH OF LOVE, RESPECT & MONEY.

VAIBHAV WAGH

Copyright © Vaibhav Wagh
All Rights Reserved.

Contents

Contents

Special thanks to: My mother Sindhu Wagh, My Sister Aboli Wagh & Shital Wagh, My wife Aanchal Gupta. My Father Sudhakar Wagh.

My close friends: Krushna Adwe, Shrikant Bhagwat, Pranav Chinchmalatpure, Ashish Kshirsagar, Vaibhav Tayde, Nikhil Patil, Harshad Mandlik, Michelle Ni, Gaurav Jadhav, Tarun kumar Das, Vinayak Kharate (Vinumama), Bople Kaku, Pratik (Maddy), Kaustubh Tikar, Nitin Rathod, Jagdish Salunkhe, Sumit Jadhao, Parag Gawande, Rahul Wagh, Manoj Kanke, Sunil Chimankar, Prashant Yarmule, Abhay Deshmukh, Sangram Deshmukh, Harsha Reddy, Nikhil Pawar, Kaware Sir, Deval Sir, Vaishnav Sir, Vikram Dixit, Sravan Kumar, Saurabh RS, Manoj Kakade, Meenakshi Sabapathy.

MAMA LOVES AANU (ANANDI) [MAMACHI LADUBAI AANU]

FUFU LOVES MEETHI & MISHTI (INAYAT & INAAYA)

CHAPTER ONE

Raswanti

April 2008

It's the summer holidays, which means No school. Most of my classmates have joined the MSCIT course to learn computers. I don't know how to start that thing (computer), but I will someday. Few joined swimming classes, and some joined the gym. I want to do all these things. I want to join MSCIT, I want to learn swimming, and I want to play all day. I guess most of my classmates must be doing all this cool stuff. But there is a big difference between what you want to do and what you can do.

Holidays mean you are free to do whatever you want. Well, technically, that may be true for other kids. Not for me. The constant worrying topic for my mother was "How to pay the room rent at the end of every month". If I could change one thing this summer, that would be to remove that constant worry. Playing all day or learning to swim might give me a temporary joy, but deep down, I know that if I could help my mother by earning some money, that happiness would last forever. And for that, I must do something different from my classmates. Almost everything in the world revolves around money. It's not just the cash that I want, but the respect that comes with it, like the kids of my age get, just because their father has good government jobs or at least a job. I have closely seen how the richest kid always gets the batting first (whenever we play cricket) because he owns the bat. The second most benefitted and respected boy is the one who is really good in the game. Well, I am neither of the two.

In summer, particularly from February to July, Raswanti's (sugarcane juice shops) get installed at chinchole chowk (chinchole square). Chinchole chowk is like the life of my small town, and you will find multiple chaats and ice-cream shops there. It's a go-to spot for all the holidays & weekends. Once in a year, a local fair having sky swings and all other rides will get set up at the place for a month or two. Apart from Raswanti's, all other radies (small street food shops) will be there throughout the year. In Summer, we go to Raswanti's quite often. There I had seen boys of my age serving the glasses, and the thought of working with them shoulder to shoulder had crossed my mind several times. That job could be an excellent start in helping my struggling family. But I never acted upon it. Besides, the benefit is, Raswanti's opens only in the evening, so I won't have to work the whole day. Well, it's easy to decide something but hard to actually do it. I wanted to do the job and didn't want to do the job at the same time. I lingered on that thought for many days.

On one particular night, while we were having dinner, I noticed that my mother was purposely not eating at the proper pace. And I understood the rest. While the rest of my house was sleeping, I lay down but couldn't sleep. I tossed and turned for ages. There would be no sleep till I sort things out for the family.

The next day I visited the Raswanti to talk with the owner. I was a little afraid to approach him. I was asking myself, will it be a good idea or not? I was strolling outside the shop but couldn't enter. After wasting 15 to 20 minutes, I managed to bring some courage and went inside. I walked towards him.

"Hello, Uncle", I spoke.

"Hello, 1 Glass, right?", He asked.

"Umm..No... Do you have any requirements here? I was looking for work this summer," I asked.

"Yes, we have the requirement. Since when can you join?

'From tomorrow. What's the timing for work'?

"You can come at 4 PM and leave by 10 PM. The only work is you have to serve the glasses to the customers.

'How much money I will get?' I asked hesitantly.

You will get 800rs per month.", He replied.

It was a great deal for me. I immediately said okay.

"Come from tomorrow then", the owner said.

I told my mother about the same. She was worried about only one thing, 'what's the work?' If it is just serving the glasses, it's ok, but you promise you won't go near the machine. The day they tell you to go near the machine, you will say No and return home. I nodded. My mother's point of view was correct. Everybody knows the incidents where people mutilated their hands in sugarcane machines.

I went there the next day. I was there at 4 PM, and no customers showed up for the next 1 hr. I noticed the lightings used for decoration; they look nice at night. I thought of having them for my house.

Electricity was taken (stolen) directly from the street DP, nice & free. The shop was standing at the corner of the empty plane ground, which was the government's property. The temporary wooden compound enclosed the Raswanti. A couple of tables were there inside. Four chairs surrounded each table, and on the corner side, there were tables with two chairs for couples. This was the whole setup. Like even if the owner decides to wrap up the shop, he can do it in no time, and there would be no trace to find whether the Raswanti even existed here or not. Besides my Raswanti, there was another one. And adjacent to that, there were a couple of street food shops.

One nice thing about my Raswanti (where I chose to work) was that the owner had kept two rabbit cages, each of them having two rabbits. That white body and those red eyes were mesmerizing, and I just wanted to hold them in my hands. I fell in love with them instantly.

I understood why the owner kept them. Cause if I had to choose one of the Raswanti out of those two to have a sugarcane juice, I would undoubtedly choose this one.

"Today is Sunday hence more customers will come than usual.

Whenever someone arrives at the table, go there & ask them how many glasses, then come to the counter and serve those to them." Said the owner. And I nodded.

Our first customer came, he was attended by another boy. Then one Family came, and I went there.

Three glasses without lemon. The Man spoke. I served them those. I was so afraid while serving because I was constantly worrying about one thing. "What would happen if I spill the juice? All glasses were highball glasses. So, there was even a possibility of me bursting those glasses on my first working day."

But No. I successfully served the first order, which gave me a small sense of pride and encouraged me to do another order. And by the end of the next hour, that one table served had turned into many tables served. I became a pro on my first day of service. According to my estimate, it was 8 PM or more because it was dark outside. Suddenly, One Family came, two kids and parents. I attended that table. Instead of drinking the juice, both kids went near the rabbit cage. I reckoned how I used to come here at this Raswanti with my mother and sister. How peaceful it is to just sit on that chair and drink your juice in the darkness; you will only get the perfect amount of light from the decoration lighting and the light from the counter. You can look at the open sky and enjoy looking at stars with your drink. I had never seen this beauty before. When I was sitting on that chair last year, I felt nothing. Probably these guys are the same.

They are feeling nothing special. I understood it then. It is when you don't have that; only then you will know the actual value of it.

I attended to a few more customers, and then a family of three came, a girl & her mom and dad. She was Shreya, my classmate. I recognized her instantly. And all my confidence of serving tables which I had gathered in last 3, 4 hrs went in vain. I just wanted to avoid that table; I wanted to hide. Too bad I didn't have any superpower. And I didn't have any place to hide. I just prayed to God, please do me a favour and do something so that she doesn't see me here. I didn't want to go near that table. Each person stays for 15 to 20 mins. If it's a Family, then most of the time, they take 30mins. My mind was calculating all that. I wanted to hide for the next 30 mins somehow. God, please help me; I was praying. Suddenly the owner shouted. "Vijay" attend that table pointing towards Shreya's Family.

Why God, why? I wanted to ask him why he did that. I just went there and stood near her table. Her father was discussing which college Shreya should go to for 11th std. I wanted to ask how many glasses, but I couldn't. After a few seconds, her father finally spoke, which was like years for me, "Three glasses, without ice". I didn't look at her. I served those glasses successfully. This time my hands were shivering more than the last orders I took. Thanks to God, I didn't fall Infront of her family. During the whole encounter, I never looked at once towards her. I hope she had done the same.

At closing time, the owner said two things to me,

1. You did well.

2. Be on time tomorrow, just like today.

But I had already decided that; I won't work here again. The incident that happened was a deal-breaker for me.

I went home & told my mother that there was no vacancy left in both Raswanti's. I will find something else. Then what were you doing until 10 PM? Why are you so late? Where were you? Mom asked.

I already contemplated that this was going to happen, and my answer was ready. 'I saw my school friends at chinchole chowk, and I played with them for some time. Later we watched all the rides and sky swings at the fair. When I thought of coming home, my cycle chain got stuck, and it took me more than an hour to fix it.' Damn, I was an excellent Liar.

By the way, if you are wondering, my name is **Vijay Sawant**, and I am 15 years old.

I never thought about my first-day salary, the work I did in Raswanti; it went in vain, just like my self-respect.

CHAPTER TWO

The Mountain of Debt

Year 2004

In summer, every afternoon, an uncle in his torn jacket and black rounded hat used to come with his ice cream tricycle cart in our neighbourhood. He had a wide variety of ice-creams, but I always had Sunny ice bar. It was the most cost-effective option. In one rupees you will get an Icey juicy orange bar. Life was simple. Schools had just begun, and I was in 6th std. Mom was nervous cause I was not in the Semi-English section. I was studying in Marathi medium. Dad assured mom that they would put me in Semi class from 8th std. (because you can't switch the medium in between, i.e., in 6th and 7th). Dad had bought a Luna 5-6 months back (two-wheeler) for his second job, 'recurring deposit job' in which he used to collect money from people and deposit it in the bank on their behalf. His commission rate was 2% on each deposit; His hectic schedule because of doing two jobs simultaneously was making the home atmosphere worse day by day. But in between all that, I was still happy about the luna, the first vehicle in our family.

On one calm evening, Dad took me & Anu Didu to Buldhana's famous go-to spot, Chinchole square. We drank the renowned sugarcane juice & ate a few other items. We then proceeded to the market. I saw a "Vadilal ice cream shop" during the journey, so I told dad to pull over. However, dad said, there is one near our house. I remembered a recently opened shop near our house. So, I kept quiet. We then went to the market, where dad finished some work. Following that, we started heading back home. As per the plan we went to that ice cream shop which was near to the house. But it was already 10:00 PM, and the shutter was closed. My face flushed, and I started slamming my fist on the handle of Luna (bike).

"We should go to the prior shop now, or else I wouldn't go home", I said with a relentless voice.

"The shop is far away from here, and we are already running late", Dad said.

But I was an adamant lad.

Finally, dad had to turn back.

In the shop, there were a variety of ice-creams from various brands. I saw a chocolate flavour Cornetto cone lying there, and I took that. I don't remember which one Anu di choose. Just for my stubbornness, dad had to drive all the way back to the market, which is another end of the city. But at last, I got my ice cream. And I was delighted.

The next day before I woke up, dad had left the town. The Luna, the first vehicle in our family, was not there, as he sold it to someone in the morning. But his cycle (dande wali cycle), the beast was still there. I was glad that we kept it. The only thing I knew was that he travelled in pursuit of a good job, which he would get in big cities. He is a graduate, so I wondered why he couldn't get it in here. Perhaps this city is not good enough for dad.

That night when I was eating that chocolate flavoured Cornetto cone, I didn't know that I wouldn't be able to see my father for the next seven years. If I had known, I would not have insisted.

As I grew up, I got to know the whole story. My father was working in a company called 'Dudh Mahasangh'. He was a 'Prashasan Sahayyak' (Administrative assistant) in Dudhmahasangh. Many workers had left their jobs since they were not paid for several months. But my father was still working there, hoping that he would get all the amount with interest all at once, and everything would be back to normal as Dudh Mahasangh was about to get funding from the government. However, the daily expenses were the same. He began borrowing money from loan sharks at a 10% interest rate to bear those expenses. And it didn't take long for that sum to reach 1 lakh. In order to repay one, he borrowed money from another. He got stuck in the vicious circle of compounding interest on his debt, and when that reached until neck, he had to leave the city. And his job as an 'Administrative assistant' came to a full stop.

After he left home, the loan sharks visited our house for many days. They used to visit and threaten us. It was a difficult time for my family. My father had also taken a 30 thousand loan from 'Mahila Bank'. So, in total, the principal amount was near about 1.3 lakh and was compounding. When compounding works against you, it has the power to destroy your ambition, your freedom and your future. My father had to stay away from the family because of that debt. I wanted to see him debt-free. I wanted to see all my family together and happy. 1 Lakh was a massive amount in 2004. And for my family, it was not just a huge amount; it was the mountain of debt. And it was my dream to conquer that mountain that divided my family.

Cycle

Year 2005

I was in 6th grade, and I wanted to learn how to ride a cycle. Most of my classmates had a bicycle, but I didn't have one. My father's bicycle(Dande wali cycle) was double the size of the bicycles I was looking for. It was resting there in the dust, and it was impossible to even think about riding that beast. But I truly wanted to ride a cycle.

I had a friend whose surname was 'Sayyad'. We used to call each other via surname in school (St. John's high school, Buldhana). Sayyad was my best friend. We used to sit together, eat together, and walk home together from school. At that time, my house (rented house) was in Saraswati Nagar. We used to walk together until Ekta Nagar square, where I would turn left, and he had to take a right. I never saw his house; he never saw mine. Maybe it was because we were simply sixth-graders who knew we'd see each other almost every day at school.

Sayyad had two brothers, and the eldest one had a cycle. So, he sometimes used to bring his brother's bicycle to school. His eldest brother was in 10th grade & had to use the bicycle, so Sayyad could only ride it to school on rare occasions. I told him that I badly wanted to learn how to ride it one day.

"Don't worry; you will master the skill in a few days. My brother won't allow me to have his cycle on weekdays, but we can have it every Sunday", He said.

"Sunday?" I said in a surprised tone.

"You tell me where I need to come, and I will teach you every Sunday", he said.

I thought about the perfect place for the whole day.

After school, I showed him the empty ground near my house. The barren land was in front of the Ganpati temple.

"That's the landmark to remember", I said, and he nodded.

"On Sunday, you come here at 9 AM, and you will see me waiting for you", I said, and he nodded again.

The year was 2005, and none of us or our houses had mobile phones. Back then, only the rich could afford a landline. But both of us had the sheer will to do the job. I didn't have a wristwatch. There was one wall clock at my house. I didn't want to be late, so I started at 8.30 and reached in front of the temple. Sayyad came in the next few minutes. My first learning session started. I fell several times, and my knees bled; the first two Sundays were difficult. On the third Sunday, I had already gathered enough confidence and knew that I could ride it without falling. Sayyad had brought bandages with him in case I crashed again as we had used mud the previous two Sundays. However, I didn't fall on the third Sunday. I rode the cycle like a champ.

Next year, before the schools were about to start, my family bought a second-hand cycle for me. They got it for 400rs. There was a craze for the ranger cycle at that time. And my classmates used to brag about how cool the ranger cycle is and stuff. Because most of them had rangers, but that never bothered me. I was pretty content with my bicycle. I just wanted to ride it with Sayyad sitting on the back seat. I had daydreamed about it, to have my own cycle and drive it double seat with Sayyad. I had already decided that Sayyad and I would go to school together on my bicycle whenever school started.

On my 1st day of 7th grade, I woke up early and got ready before time. I was very cheerful while riding my cycle towards school. I had waited for this day for a very long time. My eyes searched for my friend in the classroom, but he never showed. And the next day, another no-show.

More days passed. Things were getting a little ...strange. Later, I learned that Sayyad had left the school and I would never be able to see him again. Some said his parents got relocated to another city. I don't even remember the last time we met, maybe because I didn't know it was the last time.

CHAPTER FOUR

Cylinder

Year 2006

After my father left, every small thing became a nightmare. I discovered how tough it is simply to get the monthly gas cylinder. To book a refill, you have to go to the HP office on the other side of the town. Reach there before 7 AM, wait in line for 2 hrs, and then you are done with merely booking. After a week, go to the cylinder godown, 2kms further from the HP office. Take the empty cylinder with you all the way till godown. Then you stand in line, but there is no guarantee that you will get the cylinder replacement on 1st attempt because there will be a large crowd and not enough cylinders.

Most families had two cylinders to use as a backup when the first gets empty. We didn't have that privilege. My mother and I have been going to godown via auto for the last year, but it was not feasible to waste that much money on an auto fare to get the cylinder. We had to find out another way. I had seen people coming on their bikes and cycles carrying cylinders. They used old bicycle tubes to tie up the cylinder with their bike/cycle. But I had not seen somebody of my age doing that; they were all grown-up men. I wish I had been five years older; then, I would have done the same. I dreamed myself bringing the filled cylinder on my cycles carrier. But it was just a fantasy, and I was not getting five years older in the blink of an eye.

Getting the cylinder replacement on 1st attempt was becoming increasingly challenging, and with each visit, we were losing lots of money on auto fare. I couldn't see any other easier option. So, One day I went to a bicycle repair shop and brought an old tube from there. I was all set to save the auto fare. For me, The empty cylinder was not that heavy. I tied it to the cycle carrier with that old tube and made a knot. Reaching gas godown was easy; it was a first-timer luck that I got the replacement on my 1st trip. The challenging part was lifting the filled cylinder. It was cumbersome. I could lift it but not up to the height of my cycle's carrier. After struggling for 5 mins, I lost control over my bicycle and fell.

I put my cycle back to the main stand, picked up the fallen cylinder resting in the mud, and resumed my struggle again. One decent guy came for my help, and he placed the cylinder on my cycles carrier. He also tied it with the tube. I noticed how he tied it. His technique was unique, he didn't make any knot with the tube, but still, the cylinder was firm on the carrier. 'How can you do that without a single knot?' I inquired. And then he showed me how to do it. Then I hopped on my cycle and started the long journey towards my house. I couldn't ride the cycle with that heavy cylinder on the carrier, so I walked. After covering some distance, my hands began to shake from the strain of the load, and I lost my balance. The cylinder dislodged itself from the carrier. I was powerless. I stood back again and looked around for help.

One person was walking on the right side. But I was too shy to ask for help. I expected that he would magically come and help me, which didn't happen. I had to put the cylinder on the carrier. After a long struggle, I understood that I couldn't lift the cylinder at that height no matter how much I try. So, I put the cycle on the side stand instead of the main. That reduced the height significantly. And then I succeeded. I used the recently learned technique of tying the cylinder firmly on the cycle's carrier. The cylinder fell off more than 15 times until I reached home. And each time, it was becoming increasingly difficult to lift it and put it back on the carrier.

It took me a few trips to learn how to balance the weight of the cylinder, hold the cycle and move forward. Lifting the cylinder became easy with each trip as I got used to that weight. Walking with holding the handle was a tedious job, and I was wasting a lot of my energy on pushing that heavy cycle instead of sitting on it and riding. I wanted to ride the cycle with the cylinder back on the carrier.

And on one trip, I decided to give it a try. I waited for a quiet road where no one could witness my embarrassment. Then I dared and began riding the cycle. After a few seconds, I lost my balance and crashed to the ground miserably. The disadvantage of hiding your embarrassment is that nobody would pick you up and help you. For the next 30 seconds, I was flat on the road. Then I stood and helped myself. I was not seriously injured. Perhaps I haven't felt any pain because of the rush and adrenaline of trying a new thing. That fall couldn't dampen my spirit. I plucked back the courage and started riding the cycle again. This time, I didn't fall. I managed to ride with perfection. I couldn't keep the goofy grin off my face all the way home. I knew that I had reduced my efforts on all the upcoming cylinder trips. Now It won't take two hrs to complete the journey. I will be done just in 20mins.

After a few months, I discovered that my friend Golu lives close to the HP gas cylinder godown. Because of the cylinder stock deficit, I usually returned home with the same empty cylinder, and I wanted to fix that.

I talked with him one day and decided to keep the empty cylinder at his house.

He agreed.

Even his parents were nice to me.

Now I didn't have to keep bringing back the same empty cylinder anymore. Golu even began informing me whenever the stock for the filled cylinder was available. I was getting better at my small task. I knew that I would always remember Golu for his help.

CHAPTER FIVE

My Hometown

Year 2007

'Hey Vijay, we need to go back. We should head towards home now. It's already 8 PM', Sarvesh shouted. We three were sitting in the mountains at three different corners, enjoying the cold breeze. He was right; we needed to head towards home now. After all, we have to cross the range of mountains and valleys and then pass through the jungle to reach the bazaar, the starting place of our town, where we can see other humans apart from the three of us. I have known Sarvesh & Madhav for the last two years, and we are best friends. We all are of the same age, young 14.

I live in Buldhana, a small city amidst the mountains. While entering my town, you have to cross a beautiful ghat. Roads are really gusty and curved. As Buldhana is a hill station, you have to go all the way up to reach the city. Greenery covers the whole ghat, and fog exists almost all the time. The road is literally digging into the mountain, reaching its destination while going all the way up. One can enjoy the view of the valley, terrifying but beautiful. It's a perfect combination of the mountain's peak on one side and the valley's depth on the other. The road is you who is experiencing both the shades of life, success like the peak of the mountain, and failures, so many failures digging up onto one another, creating a deep, vast and ghastly valley. There is a Kalimata and Bajrangbali Mandir amidst the ghat. The sitting arrangement is a sofa-like structure made up of sangamravar (marble). Even if you close your eyes, you can smell the beauty of the scenery and wildflowers. The fragrance is from the good old trees and herbs which have been there for many decades. Sarvesh, Madhav & I go to ghat whenever possible. The possibility depends on whether and when Sarvesh can get his dad's Splendor (bike).

There is a point called Nalganga point just outside the city; people also call it a sunset point where you can go and enjoy the mountains and sunset. If you are stubborn enough to go down a little through the hill, you will see a small mountain stream; the water quietly flows through it, making that enchanting sound. It's clean; you can even drink it. The best thing is nobody comes there so you can sit as long as you want. Nobody is going to disturb you there. Most of the time, I go out with Sarvesh & Madhav. But sometimes I like to go there alone.

I usually go alone when it's raining. I sit there and see how the raindrops get mixed with that beautiful water stream, how they get mixed with soil and create mud. And that aromatic fragrance of the earth, I can't have it enough. Just one wrong slip of your step, and you are gone forever. The ultimate height brings an exhilarating freshness to the air. It's a divine place; It fills the void and helps you to remain strong. It is my favourite place in the world, although I haven't seen the whole world, but this is the place for now. The most crucial part of going there, apart from enjoying nature, is thinking & making plans for my future. Some of my favourite questions are:

What is the purpose of this life?

Why am I alive?

What will happen if I die by falling in this valley? Where will I go afterwards?

Where was I before my birth?

When will I get the actual job?

What career should I choose once I am done with my 12th?

Will I again miss Hindustan Vidyalay just like I missed in 4th std?

Hindustan Vidyalaya is a reputed school in Buldhana where either very talented kids or the kids of wealthy or influential people get admitted via donation quota. I am neither of those. I got 93% in

4th std, and the admission got closed at 98%.

And I know a few of my classmates, having 80% got admission there.

So, I missed it. Now the second chance is in the 11th std.

These questions that I ask myself are vital ones because they make me realise my objectives in life. Every step I take toward them will bring me closer to my dreams.

Not everyone feels this way. Sometimes the delineation between dreams and our action is a thin line; sometimes, it's a valley. But that's what makes our life exciting.

I like to walk in the rain. I would achieve perfection if only I had a classy raincoat. Which, unfortunately, I don't have.

Today, I was sitting at the same place near the water stream and it started raining heavily. I didn't even flinch. The rain should understand I am formidable.

I figured out what I wanted in life. Just three things

1. Love
2. Respect
3. Money

I also needed to draw lines on this, like how much of these are required to lead a wonderful happy life. Yes, I was quite a thinker, and I like to make plans, rules & strategies.

I made a master plan for my whole life.

It was something like this:

1. I will stay with my family and give them everything, including my time. I won't ever be too busy to not be available for them at the time of urgency.
2. I already have two best friends, Madhav and Sarvesh & that's enough. I will cherish this friendship and give my best to keep it like this forever. But I will welcome any new friend in my life while making this successful journey. Because I know it will be a successful journey.

3. I would like to have a girlfriend who will love me unconditionally and not leave me even if I have nothing. She shouldn't love me for my money or possessions. She should love me like crazy. If in future I get such a girl. I will marry her.
4. I will travel whole India once I have enough money. I will cover everything from Kashmir to Kanyakumari. I will see Varanasi & the Taj Mahal.
5. My goal is not to become ultra-rich. Everything which is too much is a curse. I truly believe in that philosophy. I need a house of my own, a black color motorcycle, enough cash to have food two times and some money to travel and explore India. That is the goal.

Although I was not old enough to draw conclusions about life, as per my experiences, I believe that Respect, Money, and Power are three correlated things. You just have to get one; the other two will automatically follow you. And when you have all these things, but you still choose to be a good human being, people truly start loving you. When I came back home, I wrote these lines in one of my registers.

CHAPTER SIX

A Promise

28th March 2008, Friday

My classmates must be thrilled that the exam was finally over. Today was the last paper for the 10th board exam. Yeah, Geometry it was! I always thought that the final paper would be Sanskrit before the Maharashtra state board released the timetable for SSC Class X. Most of the time, my intuitions turn into reality. But I was wrong this time. I deliberately took the subject Sanskrit in 8th grade and stayed with it until 10th because I wanted to learn the language. So, whenever I have enough time and money, I will search and find old scriptures in Sanskrit and read those. I believe the answer to my questions like "what is the purpose of this life?" will get answered in those scriptures.

In the last three years, I learned nothing about Sanskrit. I didn't get the ideal teacher. They just translated the para in the native language, and we crammed that to get good marks. But it didn't fulfil my desire to learn the actual language. My primary goal to take the subject was simple; I should be able to read and understand anything written in Sanskrit. I gave my best. I always got more than 80% in the subject, but I failed in my goal. Anyway, at least I am confident that Sanskrit will yield me a good percentage in 10th as well.

I was overjoyed as I walked back home after answering all the questions in the so-called final paper for the 10th. I saw a plastic bottle on the road and decided to kick it all the way home. But my mind was doing something important; thinking about my paper, calculating marks, estimating the overall percentage of my 10th and whatnot! I was walking alone. A simple thought crossed my mind, 'Holidays for two months. An immense sensation rolled throughout my body, and I jumped on the road shouting with joy "yesssss...". I will finally have two months to enjoy myself". At least that's what I thought the whole year. While I was jumping on the road, a few folks gave me odd looks, but I ignored them.

I reached home. I knew that my mother would be waiting for me to have lunch together. While entering the house, I heard a known voice. I recognized, its Ganumama. His name is Ganesh, but with love, we call him Ganumama. (My mom's brother)

Ganumama promised to bring me a wristwatch before the exam, but he was late as the exam ended before his arrival. Over the phone, he asked which type of watch I wanted. He gave me three to four brand names, out of which Sonata and Fastrack were familiar as I have seen tv ads of those brands. I remember my replies.

Ganumama: Which brand do you want? Would you prefer modern digital watches?

Me: Anything. I don't know much. Umm... Ganumama, I'd like the basic one

Ganumama: Basic means?

Me: I want the analog wristwatch.

I was not a fan of digital watches anyway. I always liked analog watches. I have waited for Ganumama for a long time, only for my wristwatch, actually. Ganumama visits us once in three-four years as he is in the military and only gets a few days off in a year.

Exams came nearer, but my watch didn't come. So, on my first paper, I had to go without it. A wristwatch can't provide extra time; that's what I told myself.

As I entered the Centre and my Exam Hall, I saw a big clock hanging over the wall. I felt fortunate.

The next day Aai (my mother) gave me a gift. Yes, it was a brand new wristwatch. The first look at that watch brought a wide grin to my face. It was a digital waterproof watch, by the way. Although I never wanted a digital watch, I still slept wearing it that night.

As I was about to enter the house, I removed the wristwatch my mom gave before entering so that Ganumama wouldn't feel bad. Yeah, I was an overthinker. Aai (My mother) asked me the same routine questions with enthusiasm. How was the paper? How did it go? and all. And I answered positively. I am always a little overconfident about myself; at least, I show so.

We all had lunch together. Me, Minu (My little sister), Anu didi (My elder sister), Aai and Ganumama.

I have two sisters. One is elder to me, 'Anamika'. We call her Anu didi and the younger one 'Minal'; we call her Minu.

That gives the introduction of my whole family. My dad had left the city to earn more money. I Don't know where he is right now. I hope he is safe and happy.

We used to be rich, they say. We had 300-acre land. My grandfather was Police Patil & was the only person in the Village to ride a horse. A servant used to bring water for him from a well which was 7 miles away from the Village, because he didn't like the taste of regular water. He never worked in his entire life & sold all the land to alcohol. My father and uncle only inherited 20-acres of land. (Which they sold later). I am not the child who is born with a silver spoon. But I always tell myself, "There is no pleasure in spending inherited money. I will build my own empire, and I don't need someone's help for that".

As promised, Ganumama gave me a nice analog wristwatch. 'Sonata' was written on the dial; I loved it. He had brought a Gulab Jamun box which everyone enjoyed. Mama left in the evening; my mom cried when he was going. He gave a bundle of notes to my mom. His eyes were teary when he was leaving.

It was a strange feeling to look at that scene. The black and white memory of my world was fading. The sky in it was holding on for too long and was about to explode at any second. I was not sad. I was angry. My rage was strangling my pain, but that couldn't change the fact that my family is not self-sustained.

That day I decided, "I will become the strongest link in my family". I will make my family stronger and self-sustained. My family would never have to rely on anyone. That was the absolute promise I made to myself that day.

CHAPTER SEVEN

Watch is watching you

April 4th, 2008, Friday

A few days went well-doing nothing like playing Galli Cricket, etti dandu, dabdubli, khupasni etc. On one specific evening, as mom and I were sitting on Veranda, on the stairs, in front of the house, mom asked, "It's been a week since your last paper. Today is April 4th; the new month got started. You have wasted all these days doing nothing. Do you want to sit idle like this your entire life? You are not a kid now. Next year you will go to college. Find some work and use this vacation period to help the family. Don't you want to do something?".

That question touched the deepest part of my heart, and I spent the entire night thinking and promising something to myself. My fear was where to begin? what work should I do. Loss of inhibition was crucial to my success.

Although I couldn't see, I could hear my new wristwatch's tick-tick sound. It was like the watch was watching me and reminding me that every passing moment was another chance to turn it all around. I don't know when I fell asleep while thinking about what I could do for the family.

CHAPTER EIGHT

Second Failure

After the failure of Raswanti, I didn't want to do any job. I was quiet for a few days. One thought was constantly bothering me; I couldn't stay quiet for the rest of my life. I must do something. But what? I needed to find that out. The next day I woke up early, hopped on my cycle and went straight to my favourite spot. My house was located on the outskirts of the city, far from the main areas like Bazaar (where I used to go to buy vegetables every Sunday) and HP gas godown. Technically, it was not our house; we were the tenant, we used to pay 1200rs per month as rent.

At 5.50 AM, I arrived at sunset point, locked my cycle and climbed on my favourite rock. I adored that place. And the rock served as my throne. It gave me the feeling that I was sitting on top of the world. One extra step, and you will fall into a deep valley. It's so deep that it will take several minutes to touch the ground if you fall in it.

The cold breeze had the power to touch one's soul. One can feel its touch on the cheek and neck while it plays with the hair. I always liked to have long hair. While I was thinking about what I am capable of and what job I would get here in my city, my hair lifted in the breeze. I ran a hand through my ruffled hair.

After some time, the Sun came out in the sky, and it soon began to shine on my face. I felt like the Sun was looking at me with a warm and tender smile. I said to the Sun, "Welcome to earth". Like always, I had this feeling like he was giving me his powers, and I was absorbing them.

When I closed my eyes, I remembered; I had seen a Newspaper agency near my current school Shree Sambhaji Vidyalay where I can distribute newspapers. I also remembered vaguely seeing a 'compounder needed' board in front of a large hospital at state bank square near my old school, St. John's High School. It was time to leave my throne.

I started heading towards the hospital. As the hospital came nearer, my heart started beating faster.

I couldn't figure out what was bothering me. But I was terrified.

I went in front of the hospital. The nameplate on the marble wall read,

Dr Deepak Naik (MBBS MD Mumbai)

Dr Suchita Naik (MBBS MD Mumbai)

It was a gorgeous large mansion in which they had opened a hospital on one side. A tiny route was built for the four-wheeler to enter, with flower plants on both sides. I was on my cycle right outside the front door, appreciating the architecture and beautiful flowers. Inside the little booth, a security guard was seated.

I persuaded myself that all I had to do was ask the security guard, "here the leaflet says you need a compounder; I am ready to work." Is the position still available? I just finished my 10th. "Am I qualified for the position?"

But I couldn't. I was scared, and I was feeling embarrassed. I didn't dare to ask for the job. How could I, knowing what he'll think of me? How can I show the world that I am ready to become a compounder? That is a disgrace.

I couldn't stay there for long either; otherwise, the guard might ask, what am I doing here? So I began pedalling my cycle. I was wandering around the hospital, making a circle around it aimlessly. I didn't want to leave the place, and I didn't have the nerve to ask for the job. I was confused. I had no idea what to do.

My heart was telling me to go there and ask for the job and take it. Do the job and be victorious. Prove the meaning of your name, be Vijay in real life. But somehow, every time I went near the entrance, my legs trembled, I became timid and bashful; I was not particularly eager to get noticed. My mind tried justifying my actions like you are too young to be a compounder. They need someone who is above 18. But I knew I didn't even ask, and the guard didn't say that. There was no age restriction on the pamphlet.

I came back home. I was ashamed of myself.

CHAPTER NINE

Purpose

As I had nothing to do & wanted a purpose in life, I decided to wake up early in the morning and run. I began waking up at 4 AM & started going to Jijamata ground. Few health enthusiasts used to come to the place after 5.30 AM; most were senior citizens. And the gathering used to grow steadily till 7 a.m. I used to get there around five o'clock and make two rounds of running & 2 rounds of walking; then, I used to sit at the centre of the ground thinking about my future.

In the morning, the ground used to be damp and cold. It does, however, feel good when you are tired. Sitting on the soil is quite comfortable and pleasurable when your entire body is drenched in sweat.

The ground didn't care about my father's position, and the soil didn't inquire about my financial status. It was just there for me. The gentle wind that dried the sweat from my forehead and neck felt nourishing.

I have known this place since 5th std. I used to walk through this ground on my way to school. Over the years, they made a few good things here, like a ten-foot climbing wall and the Zigzag track for balancing exercises. They've built one 10-foot pull up bar & two 5-foot pull up bars here. Some wicked children have drilled tiny holes in the ten-foot wall so that children like us, who are just five feet tall, might use the support and climb the mighty wall. It's an accomplishment to ascend and sit on that wall, and I enjoyed sitting there and looking as far as I can. But I realised the most important thing they built here is the water storage tank having drinking water.

It feels good to wash your sweaty face with ice-cold water. You can't compare that feeling with anything else in the world. On one side of the ground, we have Jijamata college; on another side, we have Gymkhana and Karate classes. I have attended the Karate class for some time but couldn't continue due to lack of money. In future, I will definitely do it when I have enough cash in my pocket. Anyway, the trainer was terrible, used to tell students to bring 3000rs and get a black belt of honour in competition.

One day, during my morning run, I noticed someone familiar; I bet he was "Sadashiv Aaba". But I had to confirm that it was him. As I ran very fast, I had crossed him in seconds. I was the school champion in a running competition for three consecutive years. I didn't want to stop and go back to check. I knew I could make a second round and catch him in the next 2 to 3 mins. When I returned to the exact location where I spotted him, I reduced my pace to spot "Aaba."

"Sadashiv Aaba" was 82 years old. I met him for the First Time in 'Pragati Library' (पुरगती सार्वजनकि वाचनालय), where I had been going for the past four years. The Library was free for all. It was a friendly place that welcomed everyone. You could go there, sit as long as you want and read any book you like. Free of cost. However, if you intend to bring the book home, you must pay the Library's monthly fees. It costs Rs. 150 per month. Once you register for it, they will give you a card, and you can borrow books. The general rule is you can't borrow another book while the prior one is still in your possession.

Though I was a regular to the Library, I was not a member, as I never paid any money. I used to go there daily after school. I had read the whole section of SaneGuruji, comics like Abhay, Chacha Choudhary aur Sabu. Kadambari's like "Mahanayak" by Vishwas Patil. To this day, my favourite book is "Mrityunjay," which was based on the Life of Karna. The librarian and the senior citizens mostly read newspapers. Everybody knew me in Library. I was a proud member of the librarian community & they all loved me.

Sadashiv Aaba was my favourite. He sometimes shared his life experiences and stories with me. I called him Sada Aaba, sometimes just Aaba. What's in the name anyway. He understands me. Aaba was a retired government officer who was an avid reader and a highly practical guy who knew how to live a happy life. He does not ask unnecessary questions like the other elderly folks. It's like he had seen enough life to relate and understand what was going on in my mind.

I caught Aaba in my second round. He had covered $1/4^{th}$ of the circle of Jijamata ground in the time I made one round.

I tried to talk with Aaba, but I couldn't as I was out of breath. I was wheezing.

Aaba was the first one to speak.

Aaba: Are Vijay beta, Kasa ahes? (How are you?) I am happy to see you here. So finally, you started waking up early then.

I told him I had just started coming a few days ago. We talked for a while; discussion topics started from Library and ended in our lives. Aaba is one of the few persons in the world I trust. But I still didn't tell him what was going on inside me.

I wanted to say out loud, "I am searching for a job, but I don't have the courage to face people & that is bothering me. And hence the running to find solace. At least here, I can run as fast as I can; that's my preferred way to let out my anger. That's the real reason I wake up early in the morning and come here. And when I get all sweaty and tired, those few moments give me some semblance".

"You know, Vijay, all these people who come here for morning walk are all going through some difficulties in their lives. Nobody in this world is 100% happy apart from saints, which we are not. Most of the people here are in their last phase of life, including me. Today they know the importance of health and time. But they don't have it. Some of them might have learned to live with it. But some of them haven't. It's like "Tahan laglyavar vihir khodne" (Digging a well when you get thirsty). 'THERE ARE FEW THINGS IN LIFE THAT YOU CAN'T BUY WITH MONEY' - time and health are one of them. There is nothing like the splendid youth in this world that you now have. Never say you can't do something. You deserve every single thing that you like, but you must work for it", Aaba said.

Aaba somehow knew that I was going through a difficult time and needed direction, even though I hadn't told him anything. I glanced at all those people and told myself; I have the energy, I have the time, I am not lacking anything. While heading home, I looked at myself and realised that I had finally found my purpose. I must use my freedom to do something good for myself and my family while I feel the strength and youth in me.

CHAPTER TEN

Vishvakarma

As I had seen a Newspaper agency near my school Shree Sambhaji Vidyalay, I decided to go there. I finished my brunch at 10 AM, took my cycle, and headed towards my destination. I reached the newspaper agency at 10.30 AM. It was a small office in a basement. I went there. A six ft tall guy was standing inside. I was able to see him from outside, as the walls were made of transparent glass. He was holding a tv remote and continuously changing channels. With each channel change, he was making a face. Not sure what was bothering him. It couldn't just be a T.V channel, I guess.

I had already visualized myself thinking about today's failure during my morning run. I imagined myself scurrying away from this opportunity, terrified, retracing my steps back to the cycle, pretending as if nothing had happened, and then returning to the sunset point to reflect on the failure.

No, not today. This time, I have to win, and I have to bury this fear once and for all. I was telling myself.

You can sense when a specific teacher is in a beating mood. He starts asking stupid questions to students and then beats them one by one. And you can imagine that you will be next; your turn will come in some time. At such times I always stay calm and tell myself one thing. What will he do? Beat me? How much will he beat? He can't kill me. He will just beat for 30 seconds max, and it will be over. And this thought gives me courage. In a similar vein, I asked myself, "What would this six-foot man do?"

He'll look down on me and say, "there's no work here; get lost" if he can.

That's all.

I locked my gaze on the glass door for a few seconds. "Push" was written on it. I pushed it and put my first step inside. My heart was filled with pure courage.

"Hello Sir, does your agency need someone to distribute papers for you. I am willing to do that job if there is a vacancy". I asked in a monotonous tone like I was a machine.

His eyes sparkled, and his sad face turned into a happy one. He must be looking for someone to distribute the papers, I guess.

"Yes. We have a vacancy. Have a seat", He said.

Then he took my whole interview like I was applying for IAS or something.

What's your name? Do you go to school? Which std? What is your Date of Birth? What's your age? (I mean, seriously, if you have asked someone his DOB, then there is no need to ask age, right?) What does your father do?

That question was a deal-breaker for me. I mean, almost everyone on the planet is concerned about my father's occupation. They don't give a duck about me or what I want to do in life. People have asked me this question many times. And I used to get baffled every ducking time. Because I didn't know, I didn't know the answer. If I tell them I don't know, they won't listen, they won't understand. Nobody knows how much I have suffered and struggled to give them the answer to a straightforward question.

I suppose they will never know. I have spent a couple of months getting over the dilemma. I understood that people enjoy vulnerability; they love to hear odd things. People breed on your weakness. Wherever they see a weak link, they start exploiting it. No, I am not saying all people are bad, but this is how our world works. We don't live in a perfect world. It's unfair, and you must make a way through it. If you don't, then nobody gives a shit about what you think, but if you win, then your words will automatically have value.

I had asked my father about his position a few years ago. And the answer was "Prashasan Sahayyak" (Administrative assistant) in Dudhmahasangh.

Dudhmahasangh is now on the verge of getting closed.

I liked the English word "Administrative assistant". It sounded cool. People, in my experience, automatically respect the children of wealthy people. So, the chances of people behaving appropriately with me, respecting me, and treating me well are far better when I tell them my father is an "Administrative assistant" somewhere, rather than telling them he is on a job hunt.

It took me years to learn that.

I couldn't get baffled this time. I knew I couldn't make the same mistake over and over again. I was well-prepared.

"My father is an administrative assistant in Mahila Bank. He told me to do some work this summer to get the experience of earning money on my own".

The six-foot-guy smiled. He liked the answer, I guess. He instructed me to come next week and speak with the boss.

Now it was my turn to ask a question. How much will I be paid?

He got baffled. He paused for a few seconds and said,

"The boss will decide on that. He is now on vacation & will return to the office on Monday (21ˢᵗ April 2008). You should come on Monday".

I nodded & left the agency.

21ˢᵗ April 2008

I arrived at the agency around 10 a.m. I pushed the door; it was much easier to enter the office this time than the last. A man was sitting in a chair in an authoritative position. His age must be between 35 to 40. The man (boss) suggested that I take a seat. He again took the whole interview. The six-foot guy was standing there; His name was Rakesh. The boss told Rakesh to bring something. Rakesh (six-foot guy) was a servant, just like me, I realised at that moment. And he was thrilled that day since he felt like a boss by sitting in the boss chair and taking my interview.

The boss was no different from the rest of the world. He also asked about my father's job. And I gave the same answer which I had given to Rakesh earlier.

"Come to the office at 6 p.m. Rakesh will show you all the customers. From tomorrow you can distribute on your own.", the boss said.

My job was confirmed.

"How much will I get paid," I asked.

"I pay 300rs per month to other distributors. I will pay the same to you", The boss said.

I nodded.

I left the office and headed towards home, which was at another end of the city.

I was calculating my daily wage. 300 rupees per month, which means 10rs per day. I just imagined the day when I would get those 300.

That will be my 1st salary.

I was daydreaming about the feeling I would get when I would hold that amount in my hand. My mother will be proud.

I couldn't stop smiling.

Today is 21st April which means I will get my first salary on 21st May.

As I was busy estimating and thinking about all that, I didn't realise when I reached home.

I told everything to my mother, and she was overjoyed.

At four o'clock in the evening, I went to the agency. Two hours before. The Boss was not there.

Rakesh showed me a copy of the newspaper.

"Vishvakarma Sayandainik" was written on it.

"Vishvakarma is a Sayandainik. It's an evening newspaper & gets printed in the afternoon, generally between 3 to 5 PM, and you have to distribute it in the evening", He said.

I had never heard of Sayandainik in my life before. I had no idea about evening newspapers. For me, and I believe for most people, a newspaper means the one which arrives in the morning and people consume it with their Chai or coffee. This was something new for me.

Rakesh introduced me to a person named "Pavan".

"He is our computer guy. The main guy of Vishvakarma", Rakesh said.

I looked at him. He was seated in front of the computer; that's why he was the computer guy, I guess.

He stood from the chair to shake my hand. He was about 5 feet tall, and he looked like a malnourished person to me.

I am skinny, standing at 5'2 and weighing less than a few of my classmates, but I appeared to be in better health & shape in front of him.

I was unable to estimate his age.

We talked for a minute, and then he got busy.

Rakesh advised me to sit in the lobby and watch TV.

He went to bring today's newspaper.

For the next one hour, I watched television.

Rakesh came back with a pile of newspapers.

"Vijay, come here, have a look. There are a total of 400 copies of today's newspaper. Take 60 out of them for yourself. You have to distribute 60 newspapers daily."

I nodded.

I held one copy in my hand. Each copy had four pages. It was a smaller version of a newspaper than the ones I was familiar with, such as Lokmat or Dainik Bhaskar. The paper quality was worse than the morning newspapers.

I was hoping to find some comics within, but there were none. In the library, I usually get comics from some newspapers.

"Vijay, today is your lucky day because we will distribute newspaper on two-wheeler", said Rakesh.

'All right, Sir', I replied.

'Don't call me Sir; we only have one Sir here,' he explained.

'Just call me Rakesh.'

I nodded.

I made a separate bundle for 60 copies.

Rakesh kicked the motorcycle and gave me a hint with his head & neck to sit behind. The motorcycle was "splendor plus". I reconfirmed that I had locked my cycle and then sat behind Rakesh.

He drove me across town, showing me each house one by one. And I dropped the newspaper.

"Hey, what is this?" yelled a woman in the first house.

It's a newspaper, "Vishvakarma", a Sayandainik.

"Who told you to give it here?"

I showed a finger toward Rakesh, who was sitting on the 'splendor' and trying to hide his face.

He acted like his classmate had caught him serving the glasses at Raswanti.

I was perplexed by the scene.

I asked him the same question. He was like, "Don't worry about her. Just ignore her and put newspaper here every day".

I had no idea what was going on, but I still nodded.

He showed me a total of 53 places. Most of them were big shots like the Shivsena office, SP Bangla, major hospitals, Mr Chouhan's Bangla, and other reputed houses in the city. Wherever he saw big houses, he told me to distribute papers there.

Three places out of those 53 were special, as I had to deliver two newspapers to each of them.

1. SP Bangla
2. Mr Chouhan's residence
3. Shivsena Office

The majority of the folks in the 53 locations were gobsmacked and surprised.

They were asking similar questions.

What exactly is this?

Why are you handing it over here?

Who told you to hand it over?

We won't give any money for this.

Worst of all, We don't need it; please take it back.

And when I asked Rakesh those questions, he had no answer.

He merely told me to hand over the newspaper and not say anything else.

He must have hit his head as a child, I reasoned.

The worst part about the job was that I had to tour the entire city to cover those 53 locations.

When we finished, it was already dark everywhere. I asked Rakesh the time.

"7.30", he replied.

My house was close to the last customer's house (53rd house), where I dropped the final copy of Vishvakarma. But I couldn't go because my cycle was parked outside the office.

We came back to the agency.

I was exhausted, but I had to go home.

And my home was at the other end of the city.

CHAPTER ELEVEN

The Next You

The next day, at 5.30 p.m., I went to the agency. I needed some answers.

I decided to confront the boss and ask him why we are distributing newspapers to the people when they don't need them.

What's our benefit in that? Aren't we losing money by giving them newspapers free of cost?

Because it's simple, they won't pay for it if they don't want it. However, the boss was not present.

I had to deliver the papers on my own today. I had revised all those 53 houses in my mind a couple of times.

"After the hospital, I have to take a right, then I will see Shivsena's office at the corner, then I have to turn right, then left, and I will see SP Bangla on the left-hand side; I have to give two newspapers there." I was cramming this since morning, imagining the road and turns and all those places.

It took me 3 hours to distribute all newspapers. Most of my time was wasted on answering people. I informed them that my boss told me to put the newspaper here. Some of them warned me that they wouldn't give me any money since they don't need the newspaper, which is something I already knew. So, I didn't pay much attention.

Soon it became my daily routine. I became fairly good at distributing newspapers. I was doing my job properly, but I hadn't seen the boss in a long time. My answers were pending.

The best part was that I became good at handling people and learned how to ignore them.

Some aunties were annoying. They threatened me not to drop any newspaper. So, I told them it's free of cost, don't worry. After that, those rude aunties became all nice and said nothing to me.

Meanwhile, Pavan and I became good friends. Pavan used to bitch about Rakesh.

"That Rakesh, he only has two things in his life. Watch that t.v and use the motorcycle of the boss and roam in the city without purpose. He's a puppet of our boss, so don't say anything about the boss in front of him. He will definitely tell him." I nodded.

Rakesh, too, hates Pavan, I discovered. They were the north and south poles of Vishvakarma Sayandainik. One used to earn money by sitting in the same position the whole day, and the other was making it by roaming around the city. One was malnourished, while the other was a bodybuilder. The work of Rakesh includes taking the typed copy of Vishvakarma from Pavan in the evening and then printing multiple copies at Kolte Printers, filling petrol in all of the boss's vehicles, bringing chai and snacks for the boss & giving payments for that, booking travel tickets for the boss and watching T.V. (in free time).

After working for a few days, I learned that Pavan had real issues with the boss. We shared our salary figures. His was 1500rs per month. That much money meant a lot to me. I thought he must be happy with that much salary. It's around five times what I make. He lives in a nearby village and travels to work every day. His work is to sit in front of the computer and type the news in the template. There is a pre-made template for our newspaper format. He has to update the date and the content in it every day. His working hours were from 9 a.m. to 6 p.m.

I had also seen an unusual thing: if some part of the template is empty, such as if we didn't have any news, then the boss used to tell him (over the phone) to fill it with health tips. And he stuffs it with generic garbage. Sometimes I even saw him filling the space with old news (with changed names). That was a shocker to me. From a customer's point of view, I don't believe anybody will ever think that the news they are reading is four years old. When I saw it happening with my own eyes, I couldn't stop laughing.

After that day, He started calling me while doing the filling garbage stuff.

For the astrology column, he used to ask, "do you want to change the future for Vrishabh Rashi" and I was like, "Yeah, I do. "

We wrote whatever we felt like writing at that time, depending on our mood.

I feel pity for those who believe in astrology and take decisions on the basis of astrology columns in newspapers. I hope they know how we fill the column.

Pavan had completed a typing class; after that, he was able to type the Marathi alphabet, and that's how he was able to type the news in Marathi for our Vishvakarma Sayandainik.

One thing I admired in Pavan was his 1500rs per month salary. And I thought that's the advantage of mastering an art; now he just has to sit in an AC room and type, while I have to roam the entire city for 300rs.

The next day I asked Pavan about the fee for the typing class he did.

"It's 1200rs for a 4-month course", he said.

I thought about becoming Pavan. I saw myself sitting in that chair and typing for another newspaper agency the whole day.

For calculation's sake, I can become independent with this plan. I could take a single room on rent in Buldhana, which will cost 500rs. All remaining requirements will be met in the next 500rs. And I'd be able to save 500 rs per month. Looking at it in that way was great. Pavan must be a lucky person, as he didn't have to pay rent because he lives in the village. In addition, the cost of living in the village must be lower than in Buldhana. I was all ready to become the next Pavan in my fantasy world. It all seemed nice, according to my estimation.

The next "you" is created based on what actions you do today. The hard truth in life is "Your surroundings influence your behaviour and habit. You become like your surroundings one day". Many people disagree with this statement because they want to believe that they somehow possess a stronger will and control over themselves & they won't change because of the company. But everybody knows how people start drinking and smoking. Even the strongest of rocks change shape in the water stream. It's the company that affects the behaviour; behaviour makes habits and habits decide the future.

If I become Pavan, I will get those 1500rs, but I will have to live like him. He has been chewing gutkha since childhood. That's probably one of the reasons for his short height and malnourished body. I didn't want to be only 5 feet tall when I turned 25. No, never. And I didn't want to do that mechanical job of just typing the content without using my brain. He only used his brain when there was a vacant place in the template and the boss didn't have the news which could fit there. The job was no fun. It was 9 hours of sheer labour.

On one random evening, I asked him a question I'd been meaning to ask for a long time.

"Are you happy with your job Pavan?"

And he poured his heart out to me.

"Vijay, there is not a single day that passes without me thinking about running away from this godforsaken place".

He abused the boss and blamed him for not giving him enough money. He blamed the boss for asking him to come to work on a holiday. He also told about his back pain. His words were filled with anguish and suffering.

"Vijay, it's not easy to sit in this chair all day and type. The work is so monotonous. I can't rest because I have to fill the paper before 6 PM; otherwise, it won't get printed in time, and the boss will yell. I have practised typing the Marathi alphabet on this English keyboard; it didn't happen overnight. I practised for years. In the beginning, it took me a lot of time to do the same job. I had to put up with the boss's abuse and scolding. At the very least, I now have some command and will be able to finish on time. Nowadays, I am able to complete the work before 5 PM & that's why I can leave an hour earlier. Sitting in this small room is suffocating, but I have no choice because no one in my village will pay me 1500rs for a sitting job. Other labourers in my village work all day on the farm. Working in the sun is not easy. And after all the hard work, they only get 60rs at the end of the day. I couldn't do that kind of labour. I guess I'm doing far better than those guys."

After hearing that, I was stunned. I could feel his pain.

I had never imagined this aspect of his life before. I didn't count his travelling time, although he won't have to pay for it (as the boss pays for his travelling pass). However, his time is getting consumed every day by travelling. And time is money. I didn't think about his family responsibilities and the expenses for the same.

My Class X result will be out in a month or two, and college will begin. Then I won't have an entire day to sit in one spot and type for the newspaper. Besides, I don't have 1200rs and four months to complete the typing class. I guess I had already decided that becoming the next Pavan won't be my future. I didn't want that future; hence, my mind was searching for valid reasons not to work in that direction.

I decided that I would not become the next Rakesh or Pavan. I was well aware of how different they were. But I saw the common things in them.

Both were uneducated. Rakesh failed in 10th grade, and Pavan dropped out of school in 6th. "We are all self-made. It's the decisions we make today that decide what lies in our future". But those who couldn't do much in life won't agree with this because they love to blame fate for their mistakes. However, successful people tend to agree with this since they want to take credit for their achievements.

Both philosophies are flawed. A successful life requires both hard work and good fortune.

Rakesh and Pavan will never agree that it's their mistakes and decisions they made ten years ago that brought them here. Pavan might be blaming his boss today, which in a way is right, but the real culprit was Pavan himself. He didn't complete his education; he didn't master any new thing for business setup or something.

Otherwise, he would have been in a very different position today. I realised that people are working at jobs they hate. 9hrs a day means it's where you spend the majority of your time. If you are in a situation that you are not happy with, then you only have two choices. Change the circumstances, or endure it. And if you're staying but you don't want to be there, you must leave that situation and trust that there is something better out there.

But I can't say it because that will hurt their feelings. Besides, I am nobody; I distribute newspapers and earn way less than both. To me, they are seniors. So, I just have to shut my mouth and keep my thoughts to myself. This is just a part-time job for me. I will not commit to any such duty that will consume my entire day because that will directly hinder my education. I told myself. **I aspire to do more in life.**

Real World

When my boss showed up at the office one day, I knew it was time to ask him about my unanswered questions. The main question was, "Why do we deliberately distribute newspapers to individuals who don't want them?"

I had realised that none of my 53 customers had asked for the newspaper. Some of them were so ignorant that they didn't even bother to ask why I delivered it there. But I knew that nobody would pay for it because they never wanted it in the first place.

I wanted to ask him the question, but he was in a bad mood. And I didn't have enough courage to ask him. I knew that he wouldn't be visible for the next few days, and it's hard to find him here, but still, I didn't ask. I was afraid. I just took my 53 copies and left.

Later that day, I regretted my decision. How could I ever achieve anything in life if I am so afraid of everyone? I asked myself that valid question.

Luckily, the boss was at the office the next day. I finally worked up the courage to speak up and asked him the question. He didn't give me any satisfactory answers. In fact, he didn't answer. He just said, "Don't worry about that; just keep giving them the newspaper." I warned him that he wouldn't get any payment. He seemed unconcerned about my warning and said nothing about that.

I told Rakesh to take me to "Kolte Printers". I was excited. I wanted to see how newspapers get printed. I wanted to see the whole process. I imagined a large factory where several agencies come and print their newspapers. I wanted to see that entire factory, every division, all the machines and workers.

I sat on the splendor with Rakesh. We quickly arrived at "Kolte Printers". Damn. It was just another little basement room. The bubble of my imagination in which I saw Kolte Printers as a giant factory burst in seconds.

The printing machine was massive, taking up nearly the entire room. It featured a utility for storing ink. Rakesh showed me the container and said, "We have to fill this with ink after every 20 to 25 pages get printed". He added the blueprint of today's newspaper to the machine.

As the blueprint got pulled into the machine, I stared at it for one last time. The creation of that blueprint had taken 8hrs from Pavan's life. The engine started, making a hoarse noise. The machine was like an ink eater, sucking ink and putting it on one big rod. The ink was being evenly spread on the rod, and every new blank page was getting wrapped on that rod, and boom, we were getting fresh newspaper at the other end. Rakesh counted the pages from the roll to refill the ink every 20 to 25 pages. The machine had stopped working in between, and the printer guy had to remove the rod and replace it. It took almost an hour to print all the pages. Once the printing was done, we had a long roll of unending newspaper just like toilet paper. Rakesh made a fine cut with the help of a cutter. Finally, our Vishvakarma was ready for distribution.

I just looked at the printer guy, another Xerox copy of Pavan, malnourished and sad. It may be due to a lack of oxygen, I suppose. The basement room was not worthy of staying for more than an hour. I realised there are lots of Pavan's everywhere. It's not fair. But unfortunately, we don't live in a fair world. We live in this one. Here nobody cares about you if you do not have money. I realised that nobody would give you the life you want. You have to take it for yourself. I can't do anything for the printer guy; I can't do anything for Pavan. In fact, I am not able to do anything for myself right now. But I will do everything I can to make it a better place for myself and my family, I promised myself. We came to the office. I took my 53 copies and left.

CHAPTER THIRTEEN

First Salary

After a few days, the 21st of May arrived. It was my salary day. I went to the office with all the excitement in the world. However, the boss was not present. I thought of asking about my salary to Rakesh as he was there in the office, but I didn't. I just took my 53 copies and left. The next day, even Rakesh was not there.

The whole week went like that. I was losing patience with each passing day. How can someone be so irresponsible? I would never have done that if I were in his position. When I eventually saw the boss in the office one day, I asked him about my salary, and he said, "I'll give it to you tomorrow." I just said ok to him. Didn't say a word. I was angry, but I didn't have the courage to say anything to him. I was just nice & polite. I wished I hadn't been so polite that day.

I wondered what to say to him if I found him in the office the next day. Finally, I made a plan. After two more days, I saw him in the office. I politely asked him for the salary and also told him that my father was excited about my first salary. He took out his wallet and handed me three 100-rupee notes. I took that amount, took my 53 copies and walked towards my cycle. I saw those three notes one more time; it was the hard work of my entire month. I smiled a little and put them in my pant pocket. I realised I was not as happy as I thought I'd be. I had visualised this day multiple times, like how cool it would be to hold the money you earned on your own, money earned through hard work and sweat. No doubt, it is a good feeling but not as great as I thought it would be. I guess I don't know what I really want in life. What is it that will bring me ultimate happiness and peace of mind? I guess I'm still looking for it.

As I was about to sit on my cycle, I heard a familiar voice, "Vijay". I looked back; my 10th-grade class teacher, Shelke Sir, was on his scooter. He was with his son, who must be hardly 5 or 6 years old.

He was our math teacher. He also took tuition for the same subject. As almost everybody had joined the tuition, I also did the same. Besides, the fees for his tuition were way cheaper than the private classes taken by big institutions in Buldhana. His fees for the entire year were 900rs. And I had only given 300rs. He asked for the remaining fees a few times, and I always told him my family didn't have the money right now. Later, he somehow understood me and never asked for the fee again. Shelke Sir is Orthopaedically Handicapped (one Leg). He can walk, but not as normally as other people.

"What are you doing here?" inquired Shelke Sir.

I came here to pick up my 53 copies. I am a newspaper distributor. I answered while pointing towards the bundle of newspapers.

He didn't say anything for the next 5 seconds. I didn't understand the situation. Have I done something wrong? I was asking myself.

Then he turned to his son and said, "Look at him, he's my student, and he's very hardworking." As you can see, he is distributing newspapers during the vacation.

I got relieved by hearing that. I was not doing something wrong then.

Then he spoke, "Bala, me tuzyakadun jast paishe tr nahi ghetle n tuition sathi" (Son, Have I taken more money from you for tuition?)

"No Sir, not at all. I only gave 300rs while the fee was 900rs. In fact I have to give you 600rs".

Then I put my hand in my pocket and took out those 300rs.

"I received my salary of 300 rupees today; please accept it." "I'll give the remaining 300 later," I said.

He didn't say a word about that. His expressions changed; he seemed to become emotional, less happy. I think he was the saddest person ever to hold the money.

He put the scooter on the side stand. He struggled to walk towards me, although we hardly had any distance in between.

And then he hugged me.

"Khup Motha Hoshil Beta" he said.

He smiled as he put those 300rs in my shirt pocket. Then he got on his scooter and drove away.

I came home and told about my first salary, but I didn't mention the short encounter with Shelke Sir.

I gave those 300rs to my mother. She gave me a teary-eyed smile.

Everyone was happy. But the reason for my happiness was entirely different from the rest of my family members.

CHAPTER FOURTEEN

Most educated person in the room

The date was June 26th, 2008. The SSC Class X examination results conducted by the Maharashtra state board were to be declared at 11 AM. I woke up early and got ready. I had butterflies in my stomach as I walked out to see my result. I knew I would get more than 75% as per my calculation. But the thought was still there in the background that I could be wrong; my estimation could go wrong. The result was important to me because it would determine my 11th-grade college. I had three options to start my eleventh grade.

1. Art

2. Commerce

3. Science.

I wanted to opt for the science field, which requires a good percentage.

My father had opted for commerce in his time. And after the 12th, he did BCom and became a graduate.

Well, in his time, the majority of the people were illiterate. Doing graduation itself was a big deal. As a result, dad had multiple job opportunities. Such as a job in the police department, being a veterinary doctor after completing a small course, or teaching in high schools or colleges. But he didn't choose any of that. He wanted to become a Class 1 officer. He couldn't achieve that and finally had to join Dudhmahasangh and become an 'Administrative assistant'.

Teachers didn't have that much salary when he spurned the offers. But today, after Sixth Pay (Sixth central pay commission), teachers are earning way more than my dad ever imagined.

I want to become a teacher. Not just for the 6th pay, as it will be there in every government job, but also because I believe I can teach well. Nowadays, everyone wants to become a doctor or an engineer as it is considered prestigious. And why these jobs are prestigious? It's simple. MORE MONEY.

The result was going to get displayed online at 11 AM. Students who aren't too excited about the results can wait until the next day and pick up their mark sheets from school. Honestly, nobody waits until the next day for the result, no matter how badly they performed in the exam.

My mother gave me 100rs (to buy pedhe). She also gave me some coins and told me to make a call once I knew the result.

She was more excited and confident about my result than I ever was. The cybercafé at Chinchole square was charging 10rs to see the result online. I reached there at 10.30, half an hour before the result timing. A vast crowd was present there, lots of students, parents, and whatnot.

"Is this (line) for viewing the result?" I inquired.

"Yeah, you have to get in line, then they will give you the token, and as per the token number, that person will get called inside. People came here at 9 AM and took their tokens."

I stood behind him in the line. After some 10-15 mins, I got my token. The guy just tore a page, took a small piece out of it, wrote a number, and handed it over to me. That was the token.

At exact 11 o clock, one person went inside. "I will be the first person to see the result", He shouted again. This was the 4th time he was saying that. He looked at least ten years older than me.

"I got 37%, I Passed". He yelled and left the café happily. Everybody laughed.

After that, so many students saw their results. Some students were not available when the token number was announced. My token number was getting closer and closer with every passing minute. The cyber cafe owner was not ready to give prints because of lack of pages and time and was only telling the overall percentage. Each student took 3 to 5 minutes as the site was slow.

Finally, somebody announced my token number.

I told my role number.

"Congratulations, you got 83.53%", He stated.

I was happy. I smiled a little and looked at the monitor. I wanted to confirm what he said. I saw that 83.53% with my own eyes. There was no time to see individual marks in each subject because many students were waiting. I gave him 10rs and left the café.

A red coin box was placed on a peepal tree outside the café, in front of a cycle puncture repair shop. We had one cell phone in our family, Nokia's basic model. I called and told my percentage. My mom was really happy to hear that. I still had 90rs left in my pocket. But I didn't feel like buying Pedhe(Sweets). This was not big enough to buy sweets. And I don't know what is. But I just went back home without buying sweets. Later, Anu didi bought sweets in the evening. Everyone was delighted.

In the evening, I went to Vishwakarma and took my 53 copies of newspapers to distribute. Rakesh was watching television as usual. All news channels discussed the same thing: the SSC result.

"Hey, Vijay, you were in 10th, right? What's your result?" Rakesh asked with a zeal. Pavan came out of his small room and stood next to me to hear my response after hearing the loud voice of Rakesh. Yeah, I got my result today. I said.

What is it? Pavan asked. He was getting impatient.

83.53%, I said.

Woooo hooooooooooo. Both shouted in unison.

"Why are you saying it in a sad, crumbled voice as if nothing has happened? Where is the sweet box?" Rakesh asked.

It's not a big deal guys, I told.

Rakesh: Seriously? This is what you think. It is a big deal. Do you know what my education is? Do you know Pavan's education? I am a matric (10th) fail person, and Pavan left school in 6th grade.

Pavan agreed with Rakesh while giggling.

"Our boss is not here. So right now, at this moment, you are the most educated person in this room. That too, you got 83% which is not a small thing. You are a scholar", Rakesh said.

Rakesh and Pavan were thrilled.

I felt good after hearing that much praise. I was not used to it.

What I am used to is 'the look of disdain from people, like you are just another bum'.

Today was different. I distributed newspapers while wearing a huge smile on my face. I was grinning the entire way.

CHAPTER FIFTEEN

I give you my word

I wanted to make some extra money before starting high school. A mere 300 rupees was not enough. As I had the experience of distributing newspapers, I decided to distribute morning newspapers as well. Unlike Vishvakarma, people wait eagerly for the morning newspaper.

I went to the bus stand, where I knew a newspaper shop was open all day. I got the agency's address from the shop owner.

"Son, there is a complex. I don't know its name, but it is near Hire Hospital Buldhana."

I was familiar with the hospital. I had a head injury while playing five years ago. We were playing on a construction site when a brick from the first floor fell on my head. I was wearing a white school shirt, which turned red in no time.

"Nobody will tell my mother about this," I warned.

We were going to wipe it all out. But then my neighbour aunty saw me from her terrace and yelled. And the whole world got to know about the incident. That's how I went to Hire Hospital. I visited it at least three or four times. Because the injury was severe, the doctor advised that a CT scan be performed.

I still remember how scared my mother was when I was about to go inside that machine.

I was not afraid.

I thought the machine was pretty cool. I was wide awake, seeing the lights and everything. It was a good experience.

After a struggle of 15 minutes, I finally found the complex near Hire Hospital. When I reached the agency, two people were verbally fighting with each other. I didn't disturb them, and I heard the whole conversation. I discovered that the person sitting inside was the agency's owner. He opens the agency at 6 AM, and the next person is a newspaper dealer, who buys the newspapers from the owner and distributes them for a profit of 50 paise to one rupee per newspaper. That was a lot of information, but that's how they were fighting while revealing everything to me.

The dealer, "Damodar," had not paid the owner in several days, and the owner refused to provide more newspapers until the debt was paid.

After the fight, the dealer "Damodar" exited the shop and walked to his cycle. Perhaps it wasn't the best time to talk to him, but I wasn't in the mood to worry about his temperament. I approached him and said, "Hi, I have experience in distributing newspapers; do you need someone to do it for you?"

His expression changed. "Of course, come over here away from the shop, and I'll tell you everything."

I detected a cunningness in his behaviour.

" You are welcome to come here at 6 a.m. tomorrow. I'll show you the line. (The term "line" is used by dealers to refer to consumer houses.) I will pay you 500 rupees per month in exchange for distributing 80 to 90 newspapers. The other dealers are also on the lookout for someone to distribute newspapers for them. They don't think much of me. They may tell you that "Damodar" will not pay you or that he is not the right person for you to work for. However, don't believe anyone. I guarantee that I will compensate you for your efforts." I gave the nod.

Don't listen to anyone once you arrive at 6 a.m. tomorrow, and I'll show you the line. Damodar repeated.

"I will not work for anybody other than you because I approached you first. I give you my word". I promised him.

I informed my mother that I would also be distributing morning newspapers. I could read the contentment on her face. She must have believed that I was becoming more responsible by the day.

The next morning, I awoke at 4.30 a.m. I took a bath and arrived at the agency at 6 a.m. I noticed two kaali peelis (Taxis) parked nearby, and two people were carrying large bundles of newspaper from the kaali-peeli and placing them at the counter. I noticed the owner sitting at the counter. Damodar was also there. He fought with the owner once again and eventually convinced him to give him the newspapers. There were so many other dealers there. After seeing me with Damodar, a few approached me and said, "He is not the guy you want to work with. He's not going to give you your money. They gave some examples as well. All of this was happening in front of Damodar. I felt pity for Damodar. How can someone be so weak that no one respects him? Those people were behaving exactly the same as Damodar described yesterday.

"I decided to work for Damodar, and I will work for him," I told them all.

"You'll regret it the day he doesn't pay you," one of them said.

"I'll handle it on my own. I had given him my word, and I will keep it", I responded.

CHAPTER SIXTEEN

Paperboy

Damodar showed me a total of 84 houses. The line was much more complicated than the one I distribute in the evening for Vishwakarma. I also need to remember which newspaper is for which house. I had five different newspapers: Lokmat, The Hitavada, Dainik Bhaskar, Loksatta and Deshonnati.

I was the second person working under Damodar at the time. The other guy was Sarang.

Damodar had a total of 250 houses (customers). At least that's what he told me.

In our days start, we three (Damodar, Sarang & me) used to sit in one corner to count and distribute newspapers amongst ourselves. Damodar taught me how to wrap the newspaper without folding it, and then he used to put a rubber on it. He was just rolling the newspaper and putting rubber on it.

Damodar shared some important information and tactics he learned during his ten-year career as a paperboy.

"There is no need to give the newspaper in hand to people. Just throw it from the outside. But make sure there is no water or anything in front of the house. The struggle comes in the rainy season. If you feel the place is wet and throwing the newspaper will somehow damage it, then, in that case, you must carefully place it inside. Also, you don't always have to climb all the floors; simply throw the newspaper into their balconies wherever possible. Today I will show you such houses and how to throw the roll. One last thing, always keep a plastic cover with you so that the newspapers won't get damaged even if it's raining. Wrap all the papers in it & you will be ready for all seasons."

He showed me his plastic cover and how he had all the newspapers arranged inside. Then he gave me a few rubbers and told me to roll one Hitavada, four Loksatta and one Dainik Bhaskar.

"You will become a pro soon". He told.

Damodar showed me the line for two days. One of the customers used to live on the third floor. Damodar threw the newspaper, which landed perfectly in his gallery. In another building, We had one more customer on the second floor, so he gave me the chance to show my skills. There was no gallery for that flat. The window was tiny, and I had to make the paper go through it. It took me four attempts to complete the task. I was wondering if he could do that in the first attempt. There was one house on the 4th floor, but there was no visible window or gallery, so we climbed those four floors. "If you're wondering why we can't use the lift, it's because there isn't one," Damodar quipped.

The flat system was very new for a small city like Buldhana. Hence there were only a few apartments. Having the fourth floor was exceptionally rare. Most customers were on the ground floor, and the few who were on the first floor were easy ones because there was so much open space that your throw couldn't go wrong unless you had a willy-nilly throw. I crammed the newspaper required for each house.

Damodar: Today is the second day I'm showing you the line; starting tomorrow, you must distribute on your own.

Me: Okay.

Damodar: You only have 84 houses in your line. Do you know how much I distribute?

Me: No

Damodar: I cover nearly 300 houses.

Me: Ohh, okay.

At this point, I knew he was lying because he said he had a total of 250 houses the day before. And I knew there was another person who worked for him. But I didn't say anything to him. It is an adventure to watch someone lie when you already know the truth. I began distributing newspapers on my own on the third day.

I was delivering newspapers twice a day, in the morning for Damodar and the evening for the Vishvakarma agency.

While distributing my evening newspaper at the home of Mr Chouhan (one of the richest people in the country and Chairman of a leading bank in India), Mrs Chouhan inquired, "Do you go to school?"

"Yes. I just got my result for 10th std, and I will be enrolling in 11th grade soon, "I responded.

"What was your result for 10th?" I knew that question was going to come.

"83.53%", I replied.

"You are a prodigy". She was genuinely happy about my marks.

She called her son.

"See how he works and brings good marks as well. Learn something from him", She told him.

"Would you like something to eat, son?"

"No aunty, thanks", I replied quickly.

"Do you want juice or something light? Fruits perhaps"

I again denied it.

This was the first time somebody was giving me this much respect for my work. I gave the newspapers and left.

I got similar experiences while I was distributing morning newspapers.

Three to four people praised me for my work.

One of them said, "Your willingness to work will take you so much forward in life, but don't sacrifice education for this. Manage both".

In my evening newspaper distribution, Mrs Chouhan was the only one who showed respect to me because most people didn't want that newspaper. But in morning newspaper distribution, where people used to wait for the newspaper, I met many good people. They were all well-wishers and treated me with respect. This was the first time in my life I realised that people respect working guys, and no work is small. There is nothing to be ashamed of about your position or what job you do. Doing Hard work to get the things you want has far more joy in it rather than taking help from someone.

In just a few days, People started liking me, I became their favourite, and we started greeting each other with Good morning. The majority of the customers were elderly people who had seen it all.

Just like Sada Aaba. Some used to invite me to tea. But I always denied it by saying I have to finish lots of newspapers & I will get late. I had a valid reason to tell.

When I think back on the Raswanti incident, I laugh about how foolish I was. There was nothing to be ashamed of. If today's me could go back in time to that day in the same situation, I would confidently hand the glasses to each of them and look straight in their eyes. With my newfound knowledge and confidence, I believe I truly became the perfect Paperboy.

CHAPTER SEVENTEEN

Forever

When I think of summer, few things come in front of my eyes, Holidays, freedom, Mangoes, Raswanti's and Ice Gola. But now I am seeing the negative side of the season. My most difficult time distributing newspapers is between 11 and 12. The sun appears exactly on top of the head and becomes as angry as it can. It's difficult to ride a bicycle when your entire body is drenched in sweat. But the real pleasure comes afterwards when you take a cold bath.

As usual, I began my day with brand new zeal, which appears to be less than what I was carrying yesterday. I looked at the sky, where the clouds had gone from slate to black. There were ominous dark clouds gathering overhead. I could feel the sudden change in weather.

As usual, I had extra plastic bags to cover the newspapers. I always see rain as a shower of blessings. The drops of water, wherever they touch, they make that thing beautiful. Those drops wash all the dirt from the roads and make them clean; the trees look greener and more attractive. Soil becomes fragrant.

The rain began to fall heavily around 12 o'clock in the afternoon, and I was standing in front of a three-story building. I had to deliver "The Hitavada" there. I remembered myself standing at the same corner yesterday when the sun was scorching. I was tired and thirsty. All my clothes were wet with sweat, and I just wanted to finish the line and go home as soon as possible. Today, at the same time and in the same place, the rain of blessings is falling on me. I am not tired at all. My hands look cleaner and more powerful than ever, even after finishing 60 homes out of 84. This is not my doing. It must be him.

I looked at the clean road from the corner where I was standing. The rain was washing all the trees and buildings. I believed it must be cleaning something more than just my body when it was falling on me. Then I looked towards the third-floor balcony for a few seconds without blinking to make a perfect aim. I quickly took out the already rolled Hitavada newspaper from the plastic cover and threw it the next second because I didn't want it to get damaged in the rain. The newspaper went straight inside through the opened balcony door. The customer came onto the balcony holding a cup of coffee or tea. Whatever the drink was, it was hot, as I could see the vapours from the road.

"I thought you won't come today. Thannnkkk youuuuuu for the newspaper", he shouted.

As a response, I just waved a hand.

"You can come inside; it's raining heavily." He shouted again.

"No, I am good", I shouted back so that he could hear me.

His kindness reminded me of an incident a few years ago when I was walking home from school, and it began to rain heavily, just like today. I didn't have a cycle at that time, so I walked. The rain was so heavy that water was getting thrown out of my black shoes with each step. I was in 5th std, I reckon. After a while, the drops grew in size, and I could not breathe properly cause the water was going inside my nose or maybe I was just tired. So I took the support of a wall and stood near it. It was a compound wall of a big house.

After some time, a woman of my mother's age came outside in the rain and said, "Son, please come inside."

I didn't know who she was, so I refused. I thought of leaving the place. She realised I was a stubborn child who would not come inside, so she brought an umbrella. She offered me that umbrella which I again refused because she was a stranger. Then she stood next to me and opened the umbrella. After some time, the rain stopped. She looked at me and smiled. She waved her hand and said go carefully. I don't remember if she asked me any questions or if we had any conversation in between when she was standing beside me. But I felt that Love. Words can be forgotten; Love is forever.

CHAPTER EIGHTEEN

First Lesson

The owner and Damodar again fought today. Damodar was not paying him regularly. So that day, the owner stamped all the newspapers with the below lines.

"Dear Customer, the dealer had not paid money to the agency after multiple warnings. We may have to stop distributing the newspapers to your house. To change the dealer or for any queries call on this number. Mob: 99********."

And I had to speak for him (Damodar) to all the customers.

"I don't know anything about it. You can contact Damodar or the agency for the same" I got irritated saying the same stuff 50 plus times.

A thought crossed my mind. What is he doing with the customer's money if he is not paying the agency? Will he pay me? Or will he do the same with me as well? But then I remembered his promise. Can someone make a fake promise? Besides, I am way younger than him, he knows my hard work & he also distributes newspapers, so he understands the pain. He will pay me. My heart was attempting to convince me, but my mind was losing the trust in Damodar.

"Hey, it's almost 11 AM." yelled a 'Lok Satta' customer.

Who distributes the newspaper this late? Why can't you give it to me before 8 AM?"

It was the 73rd home on my list.

"There are 84 houses in my line, and I start distributing at 7 a.m., starting with houses near the agency, and as your house is on the edge of town, I distribute it last. I distribute newspapers based on the ease of my route. Everyone in this area receives the newspapers around the same time", I explained.

He then gave his neighbour's example, saying that the neighbour gets the same newspaper early in the morning.

"Santosh (another dealer) delivers the newspapers on time", he said.

Santosh was another dealer who distributed newspapers on his motorcycle. So obviously, he could finish the line early. But I didn't want to argue with the customer.

"Please talk to Damodar", I said.

"There's no need. Stop distributing the newspaper here from tomorrow", he said.

I nodded in agreement.

The next day I conveyed the same to "Damodar".

Damodar: You can do one thing, Vijay. I've got an idea. You take the newspapers from the agency and cover the outskirts of the city first, then the rest.

I never thought he would say that. How could someone be so callous? Does he not know that my house is also at the edge of the city? By his idea, I will have to double my efforts. It already takes me four hours to deliver the newspapers.

"I won't do it. It will be double work for me", I told him directly.

But I realised he wasn't the person I thought he was. Perhaps others were right.

Damodar: All right. But don't stop delivering newspapers to his door. Keep it going.

I don't know if Damodar was out of his mind. The customer directly said to stop. Doesn't he get it? Who is this guy? I was asking myself.

Me: I can't do that; you must first speak with that customer.

Damodar: Ok, I will be there at 11 AM. You distribute your line and be there in front of the house at 11 AM. I'll speak with him.

I agreed.

As planned, I arrived at 11 AM the following day. Damodar arrived at 11.20 AM, and I had to wait for 20 minutes. When you wake up at 4.30 AM and spend the next 4, 5 hours distributing papers, 20 minutes feels like 20 days. Damodar talked with the guy. His condition was simple, either give the newspaper before 8 AM or stop delivering it.

"Would you finish this area first?" Damodar asked me again.

"No," I replied. I was firm on my decision.

"If you want, you can come here in the morning and give him the newspaper before 8 AM", I suggested.

He made an awkward face on that. I knew he couldn't do it but wanted me to do it. What an asshole.

At the end of the conversation, he threw the newspaper inside that customer's house and said, "We will continue to put the newspaper here; please adjust the timing for us, Sir. We are counting on you."

And he started his cycle. He also told me to get out of there asap.

The customer was yelling from behind.

"Don't listen to him and just put the newspaper here tomorrow", said Damodar.

At that very moment, I realised that Damodar was Insane. I understood why he was losing money and why he could not pay the agency.

You can't force people to buy things from you. He was not able to understand such a simple thing.

I did exactly the same as he said. The customer was yelling at me.

"This is what he told me to do. What do you expect me to do? I don't have any choice", I explained to him calmly.

"It's okay, you do your job, but I won't pay him".

I already knew this was coming. I left without saying a word.

My first month of delivering morning newspapers was over. I asked Damodar about my salary.

"I don't have the money right now, but I will pay you after five days, 100%".

I had already heard similar promises, including the ending 100%. But I remained silent.

After five days I asked him again about my money. He apologised and asked for two more days. I was getting played & I knew it. I was too naive. I was burning inside with every passing day. After two more days, I asked him again. "I've been waiting for a long time; please don't ask for any more days and give me my money", I said. "Come to my house in the afternoon", he said.

I went to his house after distributing the newspapers. It was around 12 o clock in the afternoon. The sun was angry, and I was tired and thirsty. I called his name, and he came out. He invited me in. I was drenched in sweat. My white t-shirt was so wet that anyone could see my body through it. Yeah, I don't wear banyans.

"Do you want a glass of water?" he asked as he drew a chair for me. I nodded.

His house had two rooms with a teen shade roof. That's why it was hot even inside. The walls were not plastered. But he had a big wall-mounted TV covering almost 60% of the wall. A Cricket match was going on, "India vs Australia" on "Star Cricket". He began telling me the score (which I was already able to see) and details like who plays best, how team selection went wrong this time and whatnot. I was not interested in any of that bullshit. I am not a fan of Cricket. It's not like I hate it. But I don't die for watching it as other people do. I like Saurav Ganguly and Sachin. If both of them get out, I don't watch the match afterwards. I don't care about who wins the match unless it's the world cup. It's just a game, which is there for entertainment. People generally abuse cricketers if they don't perform. I mean, seriously, it's just a match which will happen again in future. Just enjoy and get over with it. I don't know when people will understand that.

I just wanted him to give me my 500rs so I could go home and have my lunch. But I was too naive to tell him that. Do you have a connection at home? (Channel connection). He asked.

No. I have Doordarshan. I replied.

Damodar: You should get one. It's essential to have a connection at home. Some enjoyment is necessary. Otherwise, what's there in life?

I just nodded on that. His definition of enjoyment was simple. Have a big screen and stick to it the whole day.

After a while, his sister arrived and sat beside us to watch TV.

"Only two of us live here in this small house", Damodar said.

I just looked at her and smiled. She threw a couple of questions towards me, which I answered politely. She would be at least 32 to 35 years old, unmarried, I guess, as she still lives with her brother. But I was not stupid enough to ask anything about her personal life. It was none of my concern. However, she asked almost every detail about each of my family members and me.

Both siblings were malnourished, just like my friend Pavan from Vishvakarma. That could be because they spend the entire day sticking to television. I was losing my patience, but I acted calm and polite.

After listening to their nonsense for another half hour, he finally gave me 400rs and promised to give me 600rs next month. I thought I'd never get paid today.

I wanted him to give me my full payment, 500rs, but I said nothing. I took the money and left.

While coming back home, I was thinking, "Why didn't I say anything to him? I should have demanded the full payment."

I knew the problem. The problem was that I was overly nice, and he was taking full advantage of it.

But deep down, I was still happy about my 400rs. My mother was proud of me.

The next day arrived, and the cycle began again. Waking up at 4.30 or 5 a.m., distributing morning papers, taking rest in the afternoon, and then repeating the process for Vishvakarma, the cycle continued.

I was about to complete another month of service. I knew that I would not be able to continue for the morning newspaper as the admission for the 11th had started. And the high school timing for

11th & 12th was morning, 7.30 to 12.

Whatever school you attended, whether it was St. John's High School, Hindustan Vidyalay, Saraswati Dnyanpeeth, or Shri Sambhaji High School, the timing for junior high (11th, 12th) was the same, morning 7.30 to 12.

While taking my count of newspapers one morning, I told Damodar, "I won't be able to continue working here because my college is going to start soon. And the timing for that is morning 7.30 onwards. I want to tell you in advance that in 10 days, I will complete my 2nd month, and after that, I will stop working". Damodar looked a little surprised and sad. After a few seconds, he said, "Is it necessary to go to school every day? I mean, nobody does regular school after 10th".

I didn't know about his priorities in life, but I knew what I had to do.

"I'm not sure about that, but I will attend the college regularly. Furthermore, distributing a paper once a week will not suffice. You won't give me 500rs for that. Hence I have to stop working," I said.

After that, he simply said, "Okay."

I guess I didn't give him much of choice.

I gave more time to distribute the same 84 papers in the last five days. I talked with my old friends and told them I would soon stop working.

Two out of 84 houses forced me to have tea with them. I couldn't say no. These were the houses of Vitthal Aaba and Eknath Aaba. (Aaba means Grandfather). Both were in their seventies. They both asked similar questions such as, "What are your future plans?"

They also gave common suggestions like focus on your education. I felt like I was with another version of Sada Aaba from the library. Buldhana is a city of retired people. Most of the houses only have retired aged people. Their children were married and settled all over the world, and they are just spending their remaining days peacefully in this calm city.

"I guess there won't be any 'Good morning' roars in a few days", said Eknath Aaba.

I didn't have an answer to that, so I just smiled.

On my last working day, I requested my 600rs, 100rs from the previous month and this month's 500.

"I don't have it right now. Please come to my house tomorrow and take it", he replied.

I was not happy with that answer, but I didn't say anything. I enjoyed distributing newspapers. I took the blessings from all my old aged friends and finished the line for one last time.

The next day I went to Damodar's house; his sister informed me that he was not at home. "When will he return?" I asked.

Come back tomorrow at the same time, she said.

I went to his house the next day at the same time. He was not there.

The next day I went in the afternoon as that's when he finishes his line and comes home. His sister repeated the same thing.

What I feared had happened. I told his sister that my payment was pending. Take 600rs from him and give it to me tomorrow. On which she said he went out of the station and would come after six days. I was stupid enough to believe that. I went after six days because I trusted her. I saw him outside his house this time.

"Vijay, I don't have it; please come after 3, 4 days". Those were his words.

"I want my money today," I demanded.

"I don't have anything with me today. So from where I could give you? Come after three-four days", He said bluntly.

I again believed him and went there after 3, 4 days. He was not at home this time. I realised I wasn't going to get my money from him. After some days, I went to the agency in the morning and caught him. He was not afraid; he was not ashamed; he just said the same dialogue.

"I don't have any money right now, but I will give you your money in a few days. 100%". I'd already heard that dialogue when he used it against others.

"How many times I should come to your house. I already came to your house more than 10, 15 times", I asked.

But he repeated the same thing. "I don't have money right now, but I will give it to you in a few days".

Tell me the exact date? I asked.

But he didn't answer that question.

I wanted to grab his collar and throw him out of the building.

That day I realised I was the one who gave words (promised) to the wrong person, worked for the wrong person and believed in him despite all the warnings from others.

But that day, I thought they all were bullying him. Perhaps they were duped by him earlier; that's why they were teasing him. But I didn't think about it that day, and now it's too late to think about it.

Santosh (another dealer like Damodar) approached me that day and said, "Show me his line (all the customer houses), and I'll take care of your stuck payment".

I listened to all that and left for home.

After that, I went to his house a few more times; most of the time, I didn't find him, and when I did, I got the same response. I realised I'd never get my money back from him.

One day, I went to the agency and approached Santosh. "I'll show you the line; Will you be able to give me my pending 600rs?" I asked.

I sat on his bike and then showed him the entire line. When we arrived at the agency, he just laughed and said,

"I won't give you your payment. You should take it from Damodar; you worked for him, not for me. We all told you many times to not work for him, but you were so adamant."

I wanted to punch him in the face, but I didn't act on that thought. At that moment, I realised I was double-crossed.

I didn't cry, but I felt like crying. I was disgruntled but didn't argue further. After a few days, I returned to Damodar's house, and this time he told me, "I won't give you your money because you showed the line to Santosh, and I lost my customers."

I made a promise to myself, "When it comes to money, I will never trust anyone again in my life."

CHAPTER NINETEEN

A glimpse from the future

1st May 2019

The cab was already in front of my house. I locked the flat properly, went to the basement & put a cover on my bike. I handed over my "Tulsi plant pot" to the security guard and told him to water it regularly. Finally, I was ready to start my journey. I put my backpack in the trunk, sat in the backseat and instructed the driver to begin. Nidhi, my girlfriend, was already waiting for me inside. We grabbed each other's hands.

It was 2 AM in the middle of the night, and the road was almost empty after we crossed Hebbal. The flyover was looking glamourous in the yellow streetlights.

Nidhi leaned against my shoulder. I slid open the window. The cold air touched my face, and the beautiful road reminded me of something. As I was looking outside through the window, all the memories of my journey until now were flashing in front of my eyes. The passing road was waving back at me. Nidhi's hair was blowing on my face. I adored the touch of her hair and the fragrance of the perfume she was wearing. "It's not about the destination; it's about the journey," I was truly living that line.

We reached the kempegowda international airport Bangalore at 3 AM.

It was a cold night. We had tea & Khari. When you are in love and with the person you love, you realize how quickly time flies. I shared a few of my memories with her, which I had never shared with anyone else before.

When I was about to enter the departure gate, tears welled up in her eyes, and she squeezed her head against my chest, pulling my jacket over it. She was overwhelmed with the feeling of loneliness, despair & fear. Although she knew I'd be back in 15 days. She was worried about the future. She didn't know if we'd be able to live together for the rest of our lives or if we'd be separated in a few months.

She was tired of fighting her family.

She cried silently but oh so bitterly.

'The dream of our world which we saw together has perhaps faced no greater threat than it does today. But I say this, Trust me. Everything will be all right soon. Things will happen exactly the same as I told you earlier. Your Vijay remains **strong**', I said.

Nidhi was the first girl in my life who truly cared for me. She was madly in love with me. From cooking new dishes for me (although she had never cooked anything before in her life) to washing my clothes, she tried her best, and while it didn't always work, her efforts to do her best were visible, and each of those efforts left a permanent mark on my soul. Being with Nidhi was making me feel things. She made me feel things. How could I let the world take her away from me?

I wiped her tears, kissed her forehead, and went inside.

She was scared because she had no idea how much she meant to me.

What I didn't tell her was, "I'd fight every man alive in the entire world to make her mine."

People don't understand the language of love. They understand the language of power, capability & money, and I've known this since I was a child.

After receiving my boarding pass, I was about to proceed to the first floor for a security check. But before that, my eyes just wanted to see her one more time. I found her. She was still waiting outside & I was able to see her through the glass walls. I waved at her, and she waved back. Although we were 100 metres apart and were not talking, we could feel each other by just looking. She was closer to my heart than she ever was. I called and told her to leave immediately. After I confirmed that she had left, I went upstairs. I realised I was feeling something I had never felt before: The desire to live in one place forever with the girl having a golden heart. My life would never be the same again. I had found a girl who could make me forget the joys of carefree wandering. With Nidhi being by my side, I wanted to settle down in Bangalore.

Nidhi went back to her PG. She would go to the office and do the daily work she had done for months. But I was no longer at Deloitte. After my switch to a different company, the office premises didn't have the same meaning for her as they had earlier. Bangalore city would no longer be a place with cafes and nightlife. From this day, Bangalore would be an empty place for her. From now on, the moon will be more important. She would look at it every day and try to guess her future. She would die, but she will not marry someone else. She would have to send her kisses to the wind, hoping that the wind would touch the face of the boy she loved and would tell him that she was waiting for him. A woman was waiting for a man who went in search of his dreams. From that day on, Bangalore would represent only one thing to her, the hope of his permanent return to her life.

At 6.30 a.m., I arrived at Chhatrapati Shivaji Maharaj International airport, Mumbai. Sarvesh and Madhav, my best friends, were waiting for me at terminal 2. We hugged. I was seeing their faces after one year. The promise we made on the terrace, under the sky full of stars, was that we would meet every year no matter what.

We were keeping that promise. Every year we meet and see some new place together. That is the best time of the year.

We checked-in to a hotel and kept the bags there. We'd be exhausted by the time we would get down from the mountain, and that would be the perfect time to have a few single malt drinks; that was our plan.

It took us about 4 to 5 hours to climb to the top of the mountain.

Yeah, we did follow the scenic route and avoided shortcuts because we wanted to see everything.

We found a water stream and drank from it. It was better than Kinley and Bisleri. That place was untouched; nobody was there.

I did 50 push-ups there. It was a marvellous experience.

The next day, I travelled to Nashik to meet my sister Anu Di as she had settled in Nashik after her marriage. I spent two days there. Then I went to Amravati, my new hometown. My family had shifted to Amravati in 2015 for Minu's education as she was doing BTech in Amravati. Then I went to Buldhana because my friends had planned a party for me on the farm.

When I woke up the next day in the farmhouse after the party, all my friends were sleeping. It was probably because of the hangover. I like to be in control, and I love my sanity, so I don't drink much.

I went for an early morning jog. I loved that calm place. There were no vehicles, no traffic, just trees and birds.

After some time, we went to eat Buldhana's famous Mava dish. As we drove there, I recalled my childhood in this small town. Nothing had changed in the last ten years. The roads were the same; the shops were nearly the same. I saw a guy distributing newspapers on his bicycle, and I remembered Damodar and how he didn't give my hard-earned 600rs. I recalled how many times I went to Damodar's house just for 600rs, but he never understood my position. I tried to ignore all those memories, but I couldn't. Finally, in the afternoon, I took the keys to my friend's bullet and started heading straight to his house.

"I will go to his house, shout his name & once he comes out, I will grab his collar and remind him of everything. I will take my 600rs from his throat if he refuses to pay. I am not looking for any interest. I just want my hard-earned 600rs. I will make him realise what an asshole he was. This time I will use the language which he understands. Assholes don't understand soft talks; I tried that ten years ago. It didn't work", I was telling myself.

I reached in front of his house and put the bullet on the side stand.

His sister was sitting on the veranda.

She looked like a 90-year-old woman, so malnourished that she would pass away at any second. I never imagined ten years could do that to someone. And who sits on open stairs (without a roof) in the afternoon when the sun is scorching?

In the next second, I heard Damodar's voice.

He had a green plastic tub in his hands.

There was a construction going-on on the opposite side.

The labour was yelling at Damodar. "Do not take the cement from here; this is the fourth time you are taking it."

Damodar was still filling his green plastic round tub with the cement.

The labour told him that we would be held accountable, and the owner would yell at us. However, that sentence did not affect Damodar.

"I spoke with your boss, and he told me to take it today," Damodar explained.

"No, You haven't." The owner instructed us not to give it to anyone, especially you. "Call him right now to confirm us," labour said.

Damodar simply smiled while lifting the tub full of cement and said, "Don't worry, this is the last time I'm taking it, and I won't be back." The poor labour kept shouting from behind, but Damodar had already started walking towards his house.

I noticed the half-completed wall compound in front of his house and realised why he requires cement. He might have stolen the bricks as well from somewhere, I guess. Nothing had changed in his house. The walls were still devoid of plaster. It looked the same as it did ten years ago. Perhaps even worse than before. Damodar looked malnourished, just like his sister. They were malnourished even earlier, but now they look like senior citizens. I saw his cycle in front of his house. There was a bag hanging on it, and a rolled newspaper head was popping out of it. I realised that he still distributes newspapers. Nothing has changed for him. His habits were the same, and his source of income was the same. The only thing that was changed was his appearance. He aged at least 30years in the last 10years.

I was standing in the same spot where I used to park my cycle and wait for him. But he never gave me my 600rs. I knew it was my hard-earned money, but does that amount really matter to me now. Is it going to affect me in any way? I desperately needed that amount ten years ago, and it would have made the difference back then. I pay the government a monthly tax of Rs. 19000. So, the amount I once desired, I now pay to the government as a tax every day.

God has given me more than I ever expected.

"Perhaps he needs that 600 rupees more than I do, "I told myself.

"Sirji, thodi gaadi side la lavta ka?" A sudden voice jolted me out of my reverie.

It was Damodar's voice. He didn't recognise me. He just wanted to go inside his house with his stolen cement. I moved the bike aside. And he quickly went inside. He was beaming, pleased with his victory over the labour. I looked at him for one last time, kicked the bullet, put on my goggles, and left.

I drove to the old three-storey building where I used to throw (deliver) the Hitavada newspaper. Everything looked familiar. That building, that road, those green trees, everything was the same; it looked the same, it smelled the same, it felt the same. Then I realised what changed was me.

I stood at the same place where I used to stand to take the aim and throw the newspaper into the balcony. I remembered how it was raining heavily one day, and I was still standing here and distributing newspapers.

I saw towards the sky.

It was changing its colours.

That's the beauty of my city. It's a hill station, and the weather can take a total 180° turn even in summer.

The climate was changing, and the dark clouds were accumulating.

The lightning flashed, and thunder rumbled. The wind blew hard, and it started raining.

I didn't look for a cover and stood in the same place. The heavy rain washed the road clean & drenched me in no time. Although I was standing at the same place in the same city & even the weather was the same. But I was seeing the same world from another end this time.

CHAPTER TWENTY

Do Your Best – Leave the rest

July 2008

After receiving my tenth-grade result, I submitted applications to various high schools, but Hindustan Vidyalaya was my top choice. I missed it in 5th std as I had 93% in 4th std. And the admission was closed at 98%. This was my second and last chance to enrol in Hindustan Vidyalay & complete my 11th and 12th there. I gave my best in 10th std to get good marks and ended up with 83.53%. I was happy with my result because I gave my best to get it. The result of the first round was expected today & I was very excited. I was confident that I would get admission to Hindustan Vidyalay this time. I went to the school to find out how the round went. The first round closed at 91%. There were three rounds in total, so I didn't get discouraged and waited for the second round. After two more days, the second round result was out. The admission closed at 89%. Now my only hope was in the 3rd round. I must get in this time, I told myself.

After two more days, the third round result was listed on the board. My name was not on the list. The last name on the list was Tupesh. He had 87.36%. Why God? Why?

What if I had 87%? Why didn't I get it? Why am I not that Tupesh? I had several questions for God, but he didn't answer.

I talked with a few people who were present there. "Nothing could happen now", they said. The list is final.

As a result, I enrolled in Shri Sambhaji High School. The first round cut-off was 65%.

I was happy that I wouldn't have to wait for another round.

I didn't have a lot of choices. They began the pattern in St. John's high school. i.e., you have to pay 75 thousand Rs, and you will get the coaching from the best teachers in the city. Even Saraswati school had the same pattern with the same fees and teachers. If someone wants a science stream in those schools, they must pay 75k; that was the condition. I didn't have that kind of money. I mean, who makes such rules. Did they never think about students like me?

I guess the answer was no. 99% of students join external classes for 12th, and it's a big business. I only had two options left: Shri Sambhaji High school and ZP (Zilla Parishad). There was no cut-off for ZP, and everyone was welcomed. After a few months, I realised that even the students who had 70% got admission in Hindustan Vidyalay via management quota. It wasn't something new for me. It hurts to know that someone who got less percentage than you gets the seat you deserved. Even if I tell myself that it doesn't bother me, it does.

Only two things work in this world, a lot of money or pure talent. I wasn't brilliant enough to be admitted solely on the basis of my grades, and I didn't have money either to take the admission via management quota.

31st December 2015

I was at brigade road with my friends. Hundreds of youngsters had gathered there to celebrate the 31st. Most of them were drunk.

My friends & I were shouting for no good reason.

All of us were single. Nobody had girlfriend, so there was no responsibility of being sane in the crowd. We cared nothing. Almost all the restaurants were full, so I took the beer bottles, and we drank on the road.

As we were drinking, my phone rang. Sunil from Buldhana had called.

"My best friend desperately needs a job. He is drunk and has suicidal thoughts because he does not have a good job. The situation is serious, and you should talk with him. You are the best convincer I have ever known, and right now, I need you to convince him. We all tried our best, and now you are the last hope; otherwise, we need to call his parents. I don't want him to do anything reckless today because he is not in his senses and crying continuously. I know you are good at handling such situations. Can you please talk with him?" said Sunil.

What's his name? I asked.

"His name is Tupesh. You might know him. He was in Hindustan Vidyalaya until 12th grade, and then he did engineering at PLIT Buldhana. Now he works as a teacher, "Sunil responded.

"Isn't that a good job? What's wrong with being a teacher?" I asked. "They don't give salary on time. Also, the salary is way less than what his family expects from him," said Sunil.

I understood the situation and called Tupesh. In the first minute of our conversation, he stated that despite having 87.36% in 10th, 79% in 12th and an overall eight pointer in BTech, he couldn't get any job.

At that moment, I realised he was the same Tupesh who had got admission to Hindustan Vidyalay in the third round.

I heard him patiently.

He was facing three major problems:

- Not having a good job
- Family pressure
- Ladki ka chakkar (breakup with his girlfriend)

"It's not a big deal to get a job in the IT sector, join any consultancy that will give you calls, and attend off-campus interviews. Put a resume on Naukri and LinkedIn, start giving interviews, and you will be placed soon," I told him the truth.

I also assured him that I would refer him if I found any vacancy in my current company. I talked with him for almost an hour. And at the end of our call, his voice became hopeful. I didn't do any magic.

He just needed someone to listen to his entire story and tell him that there is still hope.

He just needed a good listener to hear everything.

That day, I realised that 99%, 90%, and 75% are all the same. It would help if you were not below the threshold. It doesn't matter where you went to school or how much percentage you got; what matters is your overall personality, how you talk, and the choices you make in life.

If I had not gone to Pune after B-tech to search for a job, I would never have had this wonderful job. Everything that happened to me was for the best. I understood why God didn't give me 87% instead of 83 in 10th. I understood why I am not that Tupesh, which I wished to be a few years ago. Otherwise, I would have been the weakling talking about suicide. Whatever happened, it happened for a reason. I unknowingly followed the saying earlier. But now I finally realise its true meaning, "Do your best – Leave the rest."

Rat Race

All students were dependent on the external tuition classes. So even I had to do the same. But the real problem was I didn't have enough cash to attend all the classes. The main tuitions I wanted to join for the 12th were

1. Mathematics (Math 1 & Math 2)
2. Biology (Bio 1 & Bio 2)
3. Chemistry (Chemistry 1 & 2)
4. Physics (Physics 1 & 2)

The tuition fees for each subject were 3000rs. When I discussed this at home, I was told that I would get 3,500rs for the year; I would have to manage the rest.

For chemistry, I decided to take tuition from Ajay Sir. For Biology, I decided to learn from Vinod Sir, and for mathematics, there were two good options: Patil Sir & Joshi Sir. There was a considerable difference in their teaching style as I attended three classes of both.

Patil Sir	Joshi Sir
1. Calm personality	1. Angriest person I ever saw
2. Focus on new intuitive ways and shortcuts to learn math	2. Focus on cramming and take 100 examples of the same type.
3. Made for intelligent students	3. Made for doomed students. Even a dead person will understand and learn.
4. Completes the syllabus early	4. Always late to finish the syllabus (as per the record from all previous batches)
5. Smart worker	5. Hard worker
6. Never shout at anyone	6. Shouting is a hobby. Sometimes his voice doesn't come out because of unnecessary straining.

Somehow, I thought hard work always wins, and I wanted thorough knowledge. Hence, I chose Joshi Sir.

Physics was the most feared subject, and the tutor was strict. She won't allow anyone to sit in her class unless the fees are paid. That was her reputation everywhere. I decided that I would pay that 3k (which my family agreed to pay) to her.

Unfortunately, I will have to ask for the concession to rest three teachers for the remaining three main subjects. I believe it's the biggest burden I have ever taken until now. I don't remember how many times I prepared a talk and reason to tell them for getting a concession. I didn't want to ask for a concession, but I didn't have any other option.

Vishvakarma did give me a job for more than a year (11th std), but now when I need it the most, it's not there anymore.

Vishvakarma had closed its office, and the owner sold the entire agency. But I will always be thankful that the owner paid me my salary. Although not on time, he at least gave it. I am not sure if I'll ever see Pavan or Rakesh again in my life.

I decided to speak with Ajay Sir first. Ajay sir teaches chemistry, and I found him more approachable than the other teachers. I told him after the class that I couldn't pay the fee because I couldn't afford it. I didn't give him any reasons why I couldn't afford it and my family background, but he somehow understood. He didn't ask any personal questions, for which I will be forever grateful. He even inquired about the other subjects and how I was managing them. I told him the truth. Ajay Sir assured me that he would speak with Joshi Sir (Math teacher) and Vinod Sir. 90% of my burden got relieved that day. I realised that there are still good people in the world & they do exist.

The next day, I spoke with Joshi Sir, who informed me that he had already spoken with Ajay Sir and I didn't need to worry. It was a good day for me. After two more days, I gathered the courage to talk to Vinod Sir. He didn't have a conversation with Ajay Sir, but he still accepted me as his student and told me to come to the classes regularly. I was overjoyed, but I had no idea what was in store for me in the near future.

Attending all the classes was the most challenging task. It was extremely difficult to attend them on time because there was no break between chemistry and physics classes. So we had to ride the cycle as fast as we could to avoid missing any new topics. Most of the students had bikes and scooters. Only 15 to 20% of students had cycles. I was the part of that 20%. Also, my cycle stayed in a puncture state most of the time, and I didn't have enough money to fix it, so I rode it in that state. As a result, the tube became useless, and I was forced to ride the cycle in that condition for a month. Somehow, I made a jugaad and replaced the tube and tire with another old tube and tire, but that didn't work for too long. If you can't afford the basics, you'll have to pay far more in the long run. That's how the universe works; everything multiplies. Finally, after one and half months, I got the money to replace the back wheels tube and tire. It was my fate that the front tire got damaged after a few days. I rode the cycle in that same state for another month. Then finally, I had new tubes & tires for the front wheel. I went to the same cycle repairing shop so many times that all the labours started recognizing me and my cycle. But those puncture tubes and tires couldn't break my will to attend the classes.

After a few months, Joshi sir kept the same tuition time as that of Vinod Sir. I heard from students that both don't like each other and do this with every batch. God knows why I didn't hear that piece of information sooner. I would have chosen a different teacher for one of the subjects. Maths class was for 2 hrs. And there were two batches, one from 4 to 6 and another from 6 to 8. The 4 to 6 batch was one month behind the 6 to 8 batch in the syllabus. And the timing for biology class was 4 to 5. There were a total of 20 students affected by this. However, fifteen of those twenty were from St. John's High School, so Joshi sir promised to cover the missed part in school. But I was not part of that 15. So, we five students had to do 4 to 5 bio class and then 5 to 6 and 6 to 8 math class. We will have to do it for one month so that the topics we missed because of biology tuition should get covered in another batch. That was the worst month of the entire year.

It was a constant struggle to reach class on time with a punctured front tire. Joshi Sir used to yell at us for no good reason. Out of the five of us, two left the biology class, and two left the mathematics class (& joined Patil sirs coaching). After a month of torment, I was the sole survivor. I couldn't leave any class; I didn't have that privilege.

Both were teaching me free of cost, and I don't think Patil sir would accept me as a student in the middle of his syllabus when I don't even have the money to pay the fees. I had to endure everything, the punctured cycle, and the anger of Joshi Sir.

One day, Joshi sir showed a technique to solve a particular type of integration.

"Sir, this is a very long way to solve this problem. There is a shortcut to solve this in 30seconds. Patil Sir showed us how to do that in college." One girl spoke.

Joshi Sir's face twisted in an irritated grimace, anticipating the embarrassment in front of the whole class. He shouted at her, "Just shut up and pay attention to what I teach. If you know the shortcut, keep it to yourself and do it in college in front of Patil Sir. Don't do that here. Do you understand?"

Student: But Sir, this will save ...?

Joshi Sir: Did you listen to what I just said? Yes, or No?

Student: Yes, Sir.

The whole class became awfully quiet. After that day, nobody dared to give any suggestion on Joshi sir's teaching. Students even stopped asking him doubts. Students told me that if he noticed anyone talking in class, he would run over the desk benches to reach that student and beat him. There were several stories like that. Now I started believing in all of them. He is only 5 feet 1 inch tall and has a frail body, but he is the most feared teacher among all. I had read a few books on human psychology in Pragati Vachnalay, and as per his body language, he must have had a tough childhood. He must be facing issues in his life and is not happy with himself.

Ajay Sir was the only person who used to lift my confidence. He never made me feel like I was taking tuition for free. I was treated the same as other students. And because of that atmosphere, I started liking chemistry. Organic chemistry (Chemistry 2) became my favourite subject. Ajay sir used to take tests after every chapter and show the ranking to the entire class. Soon I entered in first 5. Then after a few days, I continuously took 2nd rank in the class. I never came first, but I never left my 2nd rank. Students started giving me respect in the class. Soon I became the well-known name in the class.

All of the students wore jeans, t-shirts, and fancy shirts. I used to wear tailored clothes. I only had two shirts and two pairs of pants. Those two shirts and pants were not of my choice. I wore those for an entire year. During marriages and functions, relatives used to give each other cloth materials. I used to get them tailored by Ramesh's uncle. He was the one who sewed a new dress for my birthday every year.

I remember I never wore anything else apart from tailored clothes. I always wanted to wear jeans and shirts. But I never felt ashamed because of my clothes. That was my fate, and I happily accepted it in my heart.

Every time I walked into one of these three classes (except physics, which I had paid for), my heart reminded me that I was sitting here for free. I didn't deserve to sit here. And because of that constant thought, I sometimes missed what the teacher was teaching. I knew it was stupid to think about that. The only way I'll ever be able to repay the kindness was to learn here, get a good job & then pay back the fees. I sometimes daydreamed about having a job with 10 to 15 thousand salary per month. 15k was ten times what Pavan used to earn. (My Vishwakarma colleague). I will repay all the loans that are there on my father's head. I will repay the tuition fees of Ajay Sir, Vinod Sir and Joshi Sir. That day, I will be debt-free. Being in debt to someone is the biggest burden one can carry in his life.

As it was my birthday, I wore a new dress tailored by Ramesh's uncle, as I did every year. Nobody noticed or said anything except Ajay Sir. After the tuition, Sir said, "You look like a govt officer in that dress. Nice". I could never forget those kind words. Probably I was looking like a joker with that deprecated old-fashioned bell-bottom pant. I couldn't blame Ramesh uncle for bell-bottom. Because of him, I get a new dress every year. Also, I enjoyed the bell-bottom trend when every boy in my school desired that type of pants. That was six years ago when I was in 6th std. Now everybody wears narrow jeans. But anyway, it's just not my time to choose the clothes I want to wear. Ajay Sir was kind enough to boost my confidence, which is why they praised me.

It was seven o clock in the evening, and I was sitting in a classroom, attending maths tuition in the 6 to 8 batch. Joshi Sir was not in a good mood. I could see that in his eyes. Although the students were unaware, that was evident in his eyes. I could sense things and read faces. And that ability has saved me numerous times.

After a while of teaching, Joshi sir moved on to more general topics, such as how good marks can make your future, how the newly opened engineering colleges in Buldhana are inadequate, and why you should get admitted to good colleges for the betterment of your career.

Then he began talking about himself.

"You students don't know my value right now. Some of you get irritated because I take hundreds of examples for the same type of question. You think you're too smart and know more than I do, which you don't. Do you think it's fun for me to shout at you every day? I wouldn't say I like to do that. My only goal in using similar examples is to ensure that you understand the concept. Even in your sleep, If somebody gives you a derivative problem, you should be able to solve it."

Some of you may believe that I earn thousands of rupees by collecting fees from you, but that's not true. I don't teach you for money. I have taught hundreds of students for free. I even helped them financially when they couldn't afford to buy books and educational material. Many students sitting here in this class right now haven't given me a single penny."

At that very moment, my heart started beating so fast. I knew I was one of the students sitting here who hadn't paid a dime. The whole class was listening. There were more than 200 students in the class. Most of them knew me from my college, while others knew me from Ajay Sirs chemistry class, where I made a name for myself on the rank list. But I knew in my heart that Joshi Sir would not reveal our identity. I knew it.

Joshi Sir: "Prashant, who is sitting at the corner, did I ever ask you to pay anything?"

Prashant: No, Sir.

Joshi Sir: "Vijay, did you ever pay anything until now?"

The whole class was looking at me. I felt so embarrassed. This was the worst thing that had ever happened to me in my entire life. And it happened on my birthday. The entire class of over 200 students were waiting for my response. There was a pin drop silence, and I knew I was running out of time, and I have to say something. But my lips were shivering. My heart was racing so fast that I thought I'd have a stroke any second. Finally, I broke the silence and spoke.

Me: No Sir.

I never thought Joshi Sir would do this in front of an entire class. If I had known earlier that this would happen, I would never have joined mathematics class. My heart cried, my soul shattered, and my entire body shivered. But I had to act as if nothing had happened. I don't remember anything after that; what he taught when the class ended and when I reached home. It's as if somebody stole those hours from me and fast-forwarded me to the new time zone.

At night, I had a high fever. My entire body was in agony. If only I could go back just a day before in the past with full memory of what would happen. I would never go to maths class again if I got that chance. Sometimes you just imagine the impossible. Your mind knows that it's not going to happen, but still, your heart dwells on it. My mind was recalling that moment in the class again and again. I could see that moment when the whole class looked at me. The darkness of my thoughts amplified my pain, and I had no remedy for it. When everybody slept, the pain and suffering became more and more intense. The tears kept flowing throughout the night. It was a very long night.

For the next two days, I didn't attend any class. My family thought I was sick, but only I knew the real reason. I no longer wanted to attend any class, But if I had to pass 12th, I would need to attend those. Otherwise, I will never be able to get out of this vicious circle of disrespect and misery. That's what I told myself.

Finally, I gathered the courage to attend all classes on the third day.

As usual, maths class was the last class of the day. After the class, Joshi sir stopped me by holding my hand as I was coming down the stairs. I didn't realise what was coming for me.

Joshi Sir: Where were you for the last two days?

Me: Sir, I was ...

I stumbled. Before I could answer, a hard slap stung my cheek, and I gasped. I was not quick enough to answer his question. At least 30 to 40 students who were crowded on the stairs saw the whole incident.

Joshi Sir: Be regular from tomorrow.

I didn't say a word and just kept walking toward my cycle. In a weary voice, I was saying something to myself as I wiped one tear that rolled on my left cheek. It was not his mistake. He expected better from me. He wanted me to grow, to be regular in the class. But it couldn't erase the fact that he wouldn't have beaten me if my family had more money if I had paid the fees. In that case, I would just be a regular student out of those 200, and he wouldn't have noticed my absence. The last three days felt like an eternity that I spent in grief. I have contemplated the lurking menaces of the future. I failed in an effort to see myself standing stoutly in the midst of them. My dream of broken bladed glory seems impossible in the impending tumult. I was not afraid; I was angry. Not on Joshi Sir, but rather on my father.

"There will be no regular tuition from tomorrow. In fact, this is my last day of maths tuition", I told myself. I was done.

The next day, I woke up early and went to my favourite place. As I was looking towards the rising saffron sun, my thoughts asked me. What will you do now? Should I change my look so that nobody could recognise me?

I kept looking toward the valley, lush green trees, the rising sun & the mighty mountains for a long time. As the hours passed, I realised that I felt different, sort of new.

"I couldn't just stop going to all classes because of that incident. And I don't think anybody will ask me why I didn't pay for the classes. Everyone is aware, but no one will speak up, at least not in front of me. And I shouldn't be concerned with what they say behind my back." I told myself.

I continued to attend all of my classes except math. I pretended as if nothing had happened. And after a few days, everything felt the same. I was becoming stronger and stronger with each passing day.

But I never forgot that moment. One thing was clear: I would not accept anything for free from anyone.

It's the rage that drives you more than any motivational speech.

If the Burning anger always comes out on a weakling, then I will become strong. If the poor never get respected, then I will become rich. If the world enjoys oppressing the submissive, I will become obstinate. I told myself.

CHAPTER TWENTY-TWO

NDA

My friend Aniket had advised me to fill out the NDA form & I had done that. The exam date was announced. It was on August 30, 2009.

It was a 10+2 Cadet entry scheme at the Air Force and Naval wings. Only unmarried male candidates born not earlier than January 2, 1991, and not later than July 1, 1993, were eligible to apply for the NDA exam. According to the NDA eligibility, there was no requirement for a minimum 12th percentage. However, students interested in Air Force and Naval Courses must have had passed 12th Class with Physics and Mathematics.

I was 16 years old, and my height was 165cm. I didn't have any disabilities. I would be the perfect candidate for the 10+2 cadet entry scheme, but the tricky part would be to crack the written exam. I heard that students start preparing for it from eighth grade. On the other hand, I learned from Aniket about the entrance form & exam.

After a few days, I received my exam hall ticket. The centre was Nagpur. I checked with Aniket; his exam centre was also Nagpur. We decided to go together. My mother didn't hesitate and gave me 1000rs. I knew it was a lot of money, and we didn't have much. But still, she gave it to me. "I will spend that money wisely", I told myself.

I inquired at the bus stop, and they informed me that the ticket from Buldhana to Nagpur costs 250rs and that the "Raat-Rani," a special bus (with special cushion seats), costs 280rs. That much fare was reasonable for a 7-8 hour journey.

As I walked away from the Buldhana bus stop, I checked the notice board for a student pass. I went back and inquired about the student pass. "The pass costs 410rs for four days. You can travel anywhere in the state by bus for four days," the lady explained.

I calculated that I'd have to spend at least 500rs if I didn't make one.

The next day, I gave her my passport photo and made the pass for myself. I even told Aniket about it, and he also made the pass.

On Saturday, August 29th, we began our journey. This was the first time in my life that I was travelling via bus on my own, without my family members. I was excited about the journey.

Aniket was wearing narrow jeans and a green-white checked shirt. Even his backpack was cool. I knew deep down that I had a good personality. If I dress well, I will look better than 95% of my classmates. I was only contemplating that in my mind.

The world had always judged me by my clothes and appearance. I never minded people doing that because this is how the world behaves.

"God has given me a great personality, a fit body, a deep voice, white skin and perfect health & the world can't buy any of that. But I can buy new clothes and ideal living." That was my way of convincing myself whenever I saw something I couldn't have. I kept the lamp of hope burning inside.

When we reached Nagpur, Aniket's cousin came to receive us. He had a cigarette in his hand.

That night, we stayed at Aniket's cousin's house. The next day, he dropped us on his bike. The exam centre was different for both of us. He dropped Aniket first as his centre was near, and then he dropped me. When I entered the classroom, everybody had already started solving the paper. I was 10mins late. I went over all of the questions. The questions were difficult, or perhaps I hadn't prepared for them, so they seemed difficult to me.

Aniket's brother showed us around the city in the evening. I saw flyovers and signals for the first time in my life. Although

Buldhana is a district place, there were no signals in the city in 2009. I suppose it could be due to fewer people and less traffic and hence the town doesn't need signals to manage it. Or maybe it's the government's fault for the lack of development.

Everything was new and mesmerizing. Those yellow lights, massive flyovers, the whole city was shining in the night.

We visited Futala Lake. For sufficient lighting, a couple of electric lamps were installed in the vicinity of the lake.

A path with granite stone paving was built. Decorative lamps, attractive dust bins and benches were present everywhere. There were many local shops selling pani-poori, kachori chat, and other foods. One person was making glowing bubbles by blowing the bubble wand. He was just making the already beautiful environment more enchanting. All of the benches were occupied by couples. Almost 90% of the attendees were lovebirds. They all were young and happy. Kissing was going on somewhere. A few lovers were engaged in foreplay.

This was all very new to me. I had never seen anything like this in my city. The surprising thing was that they were not afraid of anybody. Doing all of this in front of the world takes a lot of guts. All those love birds were busy in their own world. They didn't notice anyone; they didn't care about anyone. After some time, we left the place and went home.

Even at night, the entire city was awake. On the small gully roads, people were playing cricket. Few were playing badminton. In Buldhana, the city sleeps by 10 PM. I never even thought in my dreams that people could play cricket at night. I mean, seriously, cricket at 11.30 PM? According to Aniket's cousin, they play until 3 AM. I felt like I magically woke up in another world.

When I tried to sleep, all those images came in front of my eyes. I had never seen anyone kissing live in real life before. I was able to see all those couples.

I saw the flat system. I wondered how people live on top of one another. Aniket had expensive clothes, a fancy towel, and a toothbrush. Nobody brushes their teeth with their index finger in cities. I felt a little embarrassed for not having a toothbrush. As I stood in the gallery, looking at the aerial view of the city, I realised I had seen nothing until now, and my city is a very tiny little part of this entire creation. I need to travel the world, work on myself, and learn everything I can.

CHAPTER TWENTY-THREE

Banking

23rd Feb 2009

In ancient times, people used to bury their treasures in the ground, on farmlands or in their own houses. We've all heard stories about people finding gold and treasures in their farms and homes.

Nowadays, we no longer need to take on so much risk and responsibility to protect our hard-earned money. Banks serve the same purpose of safety and security.

ATM machines were recently installed in town. I had never seen one. I was curious about how it works and how people withdraw money from it.

It seems imaginary and magical. I mean a box full of money, the doors will automatically open, and your name will be announced over the speakers. Mr Dash Dash Dash SBI Bank welcomes you. Please enter your secret code, and the desired amount will come out of the machine. This is what I had imagined, but I'll know more once I see the real thing.

Recently, a new SBI branch opened in town. It's known as the 'SBI Sundarkhed Branch.' Visiting the main branch in Buldhana is a nightmare. It's so crowded, there will be long queues, and you will have to wait for a very long time for small tasks. That was my experience when I went there once with my dad a few years ago. It must be worse by now. I contemplated. We all know bank employees. They behave like celebrities, and the customers are their fans who are continuously bugging them. They are the legends of few words and will try to stop the conversation as early as possible. People always condemn them for that. However, if those same people become bank employees, they will do the same.

I always wanted to open a bank account and learn everything I could. Things like how to do withdrawals and deposits? What's the procedure for applying for loans? Why is everybody talking about ATMs? What is an ATM card, and how to use it? How do ATM machines look? I wanted to know these things. I knew it was the best time to open an account as the new branch won't have many customers, which means no crowd. And bank employees will answer my questions because of less load of work and no frustration.

The next day I went to the new branch. The building was new, and I could feel the fresh fragrance of paint. That means all the walls were recently painted. There were three counters. Two were for transactions, and one was the "How may I assist you?" section.

A large LCD screen was mounted on the wall.

Technology was changing everything around us.

LCD televisions were replacing thick old cathode ray tube (CRT) televisions.

It was a 50inch Panasonic screen. Aside from those three counters, they had one more counter, a customised counter, and a man in his 50s was there doing attestation work. He was also printing customers' passbooks for them.

The manager's cabin was at the corner.

After strolling through the whole bank, I went to the help desk, i.e. 1st counter.

Me: I'd like to open a bank account at your branch. Could you tell me what documents are needed for that?

Bank Employee: How old are you?

Me: I'll be 16 years old next week.

Bank Employee: (Laughing) You cannot open a bank account before 18. The minimum age for opening an account is 18 years.

Me: Okay. But could you please tell me the documents needed for the same?

Bank Employee: Any ID proof having the photo on it, two Passport size photos, address proof, and the signatures of two members who already have accounts in this branch.

Me: Is it necessary to be 18 years old to open an account?

Bank Employee: Yes.

After hearing that, I left the counter and sat on the available bench. I thought about it for some time. Should I come here after two years then once I am 18? I paused for a moment to compose myself, then took a deep breath and went straight to the branch manager's cabin.

Me: May I come in, Sir?

Branch Manager: Yeah.

Sir, I wanted to open an account in your branch, but I am 16 years old, and the other sir at the counter said I had to be 18 to open a bank account. I wanted to open an account as soon as possible so that I could learn more about transactions. What should I do?

Branch Manager: Oh, So you want to learn more about banking. Nice. You are heading in the right direction. Do you have any identity proof?

Me: No Sir, As I am not 18, I couldn't even get a voting card.

Branch Manager: You are in which std?

Me: 11th Sir.

Branch Manager: Let me suggest something. ID proof can be obtained from any stationary store. Paste your passport size photo there. Then, get the signature and stamp of your school's principal.

If you can do that, we can open your account.

Me: Sir, what about the ATM card. Will I get it once I open the account?

Branch Manager: You won't get the ATM unless you turn 18.

Me: Okay, Sir. I will bring the ID proof. Thank You.

And I left the cabin cheerfully. I will be the privileged customer in this new branch to open an account before the age of 18.

I was about to leave the branch, but then I saw the deposit and withdrawal slip bundle hanging in one corner. One person came and filled a deposit slip in front of me. Then he went to counter number two and deposited the cash there. I saw everything, including how he filled out the slip. Then I decided to wait there because I wanted to see the withdrawal transaction as well. I waited for another 30mins. In that, two customers came, but both were depositors. After another 5 or 10 mins, one person came. He took the withdrawal slip. Even I took the withdrawal slip with him to get close to him to have a better view. Yeah, it was all common sense, and I could read, but I didn't have an account number to fill those 11 empty boxes.

The guy filled the slip and proceeded to counter number three.

The bank employee told him to sign on the backside of the withdrawal slip.

I noticed that nobody did the same on the deposit slip.

I asked the middle-aged employee who was making entries on people's passbooks.

And he confirmed that we need to do that for withdrawals to validate the customer's signature.

Then I went to a stationery shop and purchased a lovely red ID card. It looked like a CID card from the Doordarshan serial 'Suraag – The Clue.' But I didn't have passport size photos. I had seen a poster about a newly opened shop where they were providing eight passport photos in 10rs. I was good with pictures.

I went to the new shop and asked about the special price.

He agreed and confirmed that the offer was still on.

The only condition was the delay.

I would get the passport photos after one week.

I had plenty of time; I was not in a rush. So, I agreed and gave him 10rs.

At that moment, another person arrived and paid 50 rupees for the same eight photographs. But he got them in 15mins. He paid five times what I did.

When they say, "Time is money," I thought it was just a saying.

Today I realised the truth behind it.

I received the passport photos a week later.

Then I went to the Principal's cabin and told him the entire story.

I didn't forget to tell Principal Sir, "I want to learn more about banking as early as possible." That line was the truth & it was convincing.

Principle Sir looked at me and smiled. At that moment, I got to know that I would get the stamp and signature.

After that, I went to the bank and went straight to the branch manager's cabin. I showed him my fantastic new red ID card.

Branch Manager: Do you know of two people with accounts in this branch?

Me: I know you, sir, and I hope you have an account in this branch.

The manager laughed. He reiterated the fact that I won't get an ATM card for the next two years as I was 16. Then he himself helped me to open the account. It was done in minutes. "You are the youngest person in this city to have a bank account'. The man at counter number one stated. He didn't realise that "I was the city's youngest person for whom the branch manager became the witness to open the account."

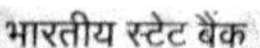
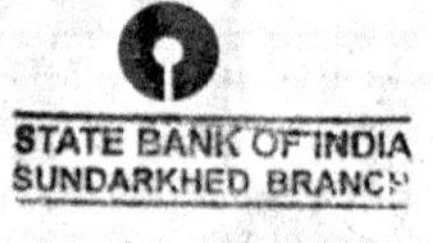

CHAPTER TWENTY-FOUR

Under the shade of Stars

Summer 2010

Sarvesh, my best friend, was my next-door neighbour, and Madhav also lived within a 300-meter radius. We saw each other almost every day. For us, the best time in the day was the evening time. My house was in the last corner of the city; there was only a jungle after that. We used to go for a walk in the jungle every evening. It was a quiet place with plenty of greenery.

I love nature and quiet places. Most students want privacy to smoke or drink and do stuff like that. But we never wanted that. We never tried that shit.

I had decided that even when I grow old, I will stay away from alcohol and cigarettes and all other things which leads to intoxication. I have never even tried eggs and non-veg. I will stay away from egg and non-veg as I feel it's not right to eat innocent animals to satisfy the taste buds.

In the jungle, there was an abandoned pipe lying there for years. That pipe was our secret sitting spot to take a break from the constant walking. We mostly talked nonsense, but somehow, that evening stroll for an hour or two became an integral part of our life.

Even Buldhana, the so-called hill station, was getting hot as it was summer. In the summer, Sarvesh and I used to sleep on the terrace. Madhav was not regular. Sarvesh and I had many fond memories of that terrace and open sky. The entire world dies to see a shooting star, but Sarvesh and I see them almost every night. It is said that if you make a wish while seeing the shooting star, your wish comes true. I didn't make a single wish in the last couple of years, although I have been seeing shooting stars for years.

But this year was different.

My whole career was dependent on two things, the 12th result & CET result. CET was Common Entrance Test.

It was a mandatory written test for admission into any Post-Graduate programme offered by the MHTCET institutes.

There were approx 220 institutes which accepted MHTCET scores.

I knew that I would get more than 70% in 12th, so I was not worried. But I was worried about the CET score.

CET was an exam of 200 marks. And to get into top-level colleges, one must get more than 180 marks. I had written 200/200 on the wall. That was my goal. But I never studied that hard to reach that goal. There were two groups PCM (Physics, Chemistry, Math) & PCB (Physics, Chemistry, Biology). People who wanted to be engineers chose PCM, while those who wanted to be doctors chose the PCB group. And then there were students like me who wanted to keep their hands everywhere. They choose both.

The exam was MCQ type. So it was a relief that we didn't have to write full answers; we just had to pick one of four options.

The exam did not go well. But I was hoping that my chosen options would be correct if my luck were right. It was plain stupidity. But yeah, now I was solely dependent on my luck because I didn't do justice to the hard work part.

Where will you go after two months? Will you be leaving the city?

Sarvesh asked again.

We talked until midnight and then went to sleep.

Most of our discussion topics were bizarre.

What will we do if a flood comes?

What will we do if our parents throw us out?

What do we want to do with our lives?

Where will we be in ten years?

We didn't know the answer to these questions.

But we knew one thing for sure.

"We should meet at least once a year, no matter where we go in life" was the absolute promise we three (Sarvesh, Madhav & I) had made.

Two years ago, I wanted to become a teacher. Some part of me still says to do D.Ed and become a high school teacher. But that profession doesn't offer that much money. So, I was going with the flow of Doctor and Engineer.

Why don't you want to become a doctor? Sarvesh asked.

Becoming Doctor	Becoming Engineer
1. Five plus years. For MD 7 years. (People prefer MD)	1. Four years and you will get a job
2. 180 Plus marks out of 200 in CET. Because doing MBBS in a private college is almost impossible. It's too costly. Minimum 10Lakh per year.	2. For autonomous engineering colleges 180 plus. But doing engineering at a private college is not impossible. The cost for newly opened colleges is 20k per year. And Even 50 marks out of 200 in CET is okay for them.
3. Your whole life will be gone in hospital with patients. Everybody knows the condition of Govt hospitals.	3. No Hospitals.
1. Do the work you enjoy. Are you that noble to enjoy treating patients? Will that give you joy?	4. Don't know the actual work. But it will be something cool like developing a new machine or something. I will create something new that other people will use. That may even include doctors.

"I don't think I will enjoy treating patients. It's a noble profession, and people consider doctors as god, but I don't think I deserve to be that god.

I don't like hospitals, and I don't want to spend the rest of my life there. Plus, I need to stand on my legs as early as possible. And engineering gives me that. My goal is just four years away. Yes, that's selfish, but it's my life. So, I will decide what to do with it." I answered his question.

That night, we saw another shooting star, and I made a wish for the first time. After about half an hour, we saw one more shooting star.

Nobody will believe us if we tell them we see shooting stars every other night. They must not be as uncommon as people think, or perhaps people aren't crazy enough to spend hours every night stargazing.

From that night onwards, I always made the same wish that I should get more than 180 marks out of 200 in CET so that I would get admission to COEP. COEP was my dream engineering college. As I was making that wish daily, a part of me started believing that it would come true.

"We shouldn't talk about the wish. A wish should be kept secret, or it won't come true. You will no longer receive 180 marks out of 200". Sarvesh told.

"We see the shooting star every night, and I don't always tell you the wish, right?" I replied.

We laughed at that for a very long time.

Sarvesh used to like the neighbour girl who recently moved into the neighbourhood. I never saw her. But as per the description of Sarvesh, she was stunning. She didn't go out much. Somehow only Sarvesh sees her. Every night Sarvesh talked about her, and I listened.

Even though I had never seen her, I knew what she wore, her dress choices, and almost every other trivial detail.

Sarvesh had a grocery store set up in the vicinity of his house, and he used to handle the customer for 1 or 2 hours in the morning. As per him, the girl used to come to the shop in the morning. They never talked much about anything other than the product and its price. However, he enjoyed that small interaction, and it was the best part of his day.

I used to listen to the same story every day, but I enjoyed listening to it. We had even made plans for the future. If she becomes Sarvesh's girlfriend, then they would write love letters to each other, which we would hide on my terrace. Nobody can go on my terrace as the owner didn't build stairs. Only I could climb onto the bathroom and then onto the terrace. Going there was difficult. But I had my personal space there. I went there to set up an antenna for Doordarshan for the first time.

We used to sleep on Sarvesh's terrace. Our parents didn't allow us to sleep on my house's terrace as there were no stairs. If the love story becomes successful, we will have to resurrect the love letters from the terrace wrapped securely in a plastic bag after many years. We had planned it all.

That terrace, the open sky, and the shooting stars, they all knew our stories. They shared our dreams; they knew what we wanted to do with our life & they will remind us to meet at least once every year when we grow old and get busy with our lives.

CHAPTER TWENTY-FIVE

Education Loan

I got 108 out of 200 in CET. My wish of getting 180 came true, but it just replaced the location of 8 and that became 108 instead of 180.

I don't blame the stars. They and the open sky gave us (Me & Sarvesh) a lot of memories that we will cherish forever. And no bed or house in the world can beat the quality of sleep I used to get under the open sky.

My focus was on the admission part. One thing was certain: I won't get admission to any autonomous engineering college.

My dream of COEP was shattered. It needed at least 180 marks. But I guess that dream was already shattered when I didn't give enough effort to my study.

Two new engineering colleges had opened in my city.

1. Savitribai Phule College of Engineering, Buldhana
2. Rainbow Institute of Technology And Management Studies, Buldhana

But I didn't want to do my engineering at newly opened colleges. I wanted something that existed prior to my birth. I also wanted to explore the world and see new places. I had already decided to leave the city and live somewhere else. Also, staying away from my family will give me 100% freedom to do whatever I want. I didn't smoke or drink, and I didn't have any addiction. I was a pure vegetarian, and I never even tasted nonveg. But at this age, I wanted to stay away from family and have my freedom although I didn't have any plans to utilize that freedom.

In the first round, I got the following college.

"MIT-Prestige Institute of Technology & Research, Amravati."

I wanted the "EXTC" or "Mechanical" branch. But due to my low marks, I got computer Science. EXTC had closed at 118 & mechanical at 115. But I was content because the college had a good reputation. It was established in 1983, and the placement was good for all the batches.

A few years ago, the Computer Science branch was booming. And it required the highest marks, but in recent years, students have preferred EXTC and Mechanical. People lost their IT jobs during the 2008 recession, and the CSE craze had waned since then.

You must have heard, "Sabka baap ek hai Mech hai Mech hai". Mechanical and EXTC were considered evergreen.

But I am a believer. Perhaps after four years, when I will be a graduate of Computer Science, CSE will be thriving again. Who knows the future.

The main issue was still unresolved. The fees for open candidates (those whose caste is open) were 80k. I didn't have that kind of money. I had to take a loan from the bank.

I met my friend Amar and learned that he also got the same college and same branch.

"It's very easy to obtain an education loan; I applied at the Central Bank. Two bank officers came to my home to look at the house. Because my family does not own farmland, this small house was the only property we could show. And the loan got approved," Amar said.

"I don't even have a house; I live in a rented house," I wanted to say, but I didn't.

I didn't lose hope. I went to all the major banks in Buldhana. All of them needed a document of property to sanction the loan. And I didn't have one. But I saw a ray of hope from Maharashtra bank. The way the bank manager had treated me was far better than other banks. He asked me about my 10th and 12th percentage. And I told 83.53% and 70.83% respectively. He was somewhat impressed by hearing that. However, 70% in 12th was not that great; it was mediocre.

"In the past, I have sanctioned loans to multiple students who did not have any property documents to show. However, after their education, they all paid their loans on time.

Come in tomorrow at 11 a.m., and if I have time, I'll call you inside." he stated.

I went there the next day a little before 11 a.m. The Bank manager was busy talking with other people. I waited for the next 3 to 4hrs. But multiple people were lined up to meet him, and I didn't get any chance. The majority of Maharashtra Bank's customers were older adults from nearby villages. I noticed that they were unable to write any form. In fact, most of them couldn't write anything. They struggled to find a pen.

The next day I brought a pen with me. As usual, the manager was busy with meetings, so I started helping the customers. I filled out their slips. Almost all of them were either deposit slips or withdrawal slips. I recalled seeing the slips for the first time in SBI.

People soon formed a line to have their slips filled by me. I believe they thought of me as a bank employee.

Yesterday was boring because I waited for the manager's signal and did nothing. When you have nothing to do, time moves very slowly. Three-four hours feels like three-four days. But today was wonderful. I stopped looking at the manager's cabin and focused on helping the customers. Few of the customers even asked me about the loan and other stuff, for which I didn't have an answer. So I redirected them to particular counters. This routine continued for the entire week. On Friday, Manager asked me to come inside. He looked very happy. I already had all of the documents he requested.

Bank Manager: I noticed you helping villagers with filling out the slips. You almost became a bank employee.

Me: I didn't have anything to do, Sir. So, I thought of helping them.

Bank Manager: I believe in your spirit of doing work. And I hope that after your engineering, you will get a good job and you will repay the amount.

He approved the loan amount for all the years of engineering. And I left for home with a smiling face.

CHAPTER TWENTY-SIX

Skill Set

We all have heard the phrase "Survival of the fittest". The basic instinct of every living thing in this world is survival. And I truly believed in that.

And that's why I made a list of things that I wanted to learn. I had a month on my hand before college (Engineering 1ˢᵗ year) would start.

My goal for the month was to learn two new things: Swimming and motorcycle riding. Madhav and I started going to "Krida Sankul, Buldhana." Krida Sankul was more than just a swimming pool. It had a cricket ground, table tennis court, basketball court, and even indoor games like carrom. It was at the other end of the city and quite far from our homes, but that didn't stop us from going. Krida Sankul had a large swimming pool, and swimming classes were held in the morning. The fee was 500rs per month. We didn't have that much, so we had to think of another solution.

On one fine day, I stayed there in Krida Sankul and observed everything from morning till evening. I saw people coming and going. But it was almost vacant in afternoon hours. People don't go out much on sunny afternoons, especially in the summer.

There were no Swimming batches in the afternoon. I made a plan to use that to our advantage. Madhav and I started going there in the afternoon. There was only one guard on duty. I spoke with him for a few minutes and told him, "The swimming pool is empty for hours in the afternoon anyway". After some more discussion, he agreed that he would allow us inside, but he will take 10rs for an hour. It was an excellent deal for us. We started going there in the afternoon when there would be no one. And we just had to pay 10rs to the guard there, and he used to allow us for an hour. It was way better than going there early in the morning, paying more and swimming in the crowd. We also discovered that nobody comes there on Sundays, sometimes not even guards, so we started going there on the afternoon of Sundays as well. We had the entire swimming pool to ourselves. In just a few days, I learned swimming properly.

It was now time to learn how to ride a motorcycle. Sarvesh's father had an old model of splendor (motorcycle). I spoke with Sarvesh, and he promised that he would teach me bike riding.

One fine Sunday, we took his father's splendor and went to the wilderness.

He explained all the basic functionalities like clutch, brake, gearbox & accelerator.

Now it was my turn to ride it. The road was not proper, but somehow, I managed to ride it even on my first day. Keeping the balance on just two tyres was simple, thanks to Sayyad, who taught me how to ride a bicycle. Without that, I believe it would have been extremely difficult. The hardest part was clutch and starting the bike with 1st gear. I tried it multiple times but always ended up in failure.

"Release the clutch slowly, and don't give the accelerator", Sarvesh said.

The next day Sarvesh managed to get the bike for one hour, but I couldn't master the skill of starting the bike with a slow and steady clutch release. Unfortunately, that was the last class Sarvesh could manage. His parents forbade us from riding the bike on unpaved roads in the jungle for our own safety. I knew there was nothing in his hand & he tried his best for my benefit. I didn't have 100% confidence to ride the motorcycle, but I understood everything theoretically.

When I left the city (Buldhana) for my first year of engineering in Amravati, I had to pick up one of my friends from the railway station, and Sameer gave me the keys to his bike. He assumed I already knew how to ride a bike. I took the keys and started the motorcycle with complete confidence in myself. "Release the clutch slowly and steadily", I remembered the words of Sarvesh.

Luckily, I didn't fail, and the bike started.

At the railway crossing of Rajapeth, I got a little bit scared.

There were no railway lines in Buldhana (as it's a hill station); this was my first time stopping at a railway crossing. A superfast express passed in a blink of an eye. I was afraid that if I lost control of the motorcycle clutch, this would be my last day on earth. I was holding my breath while the gate was closed. I let out a sigh of relief once the train passed and the gate got opened.

In a few days, I became a pro in bike riding. Although my friends assumed I was already a pro, only I knew the truth. I never cared or thought about getting a driving license as no traffic police had ever stopped me.

On one beautiful evening, I was riding Sameer's bike, triple seat. We all started to believe that the tripsy felt safer than riding a pillion.

The wind was blowing through my hair, and the weather was nice, the kind that comes just before the rain and all the green trees were going behind me.

But as we reached the highway, it was a task to keep an eye on the roads, not to meet traffic police, and if we saw one, I would slow down the bike, and one of us would quickly get down. With the winter winds gushing on my face and my friend's hands wrapped around me, I felt strong.

I put that 4th gear of the splendor and gave full accelerator; I was enjoying the ride.

At that moment, I realised that this all became possible because of my friends. When I look back on my life of 18 years, I see how much they have done for me and how little I have done for them.

CHAPTER TWENTY-SEVEN

Engineering 1st Year

Year 2011

For the first time in my life, I was going to stay outside my city. I never stayed away from my mother. I always wanted to see the world outside this city and live on my own, without my family's support. The day had finally arrived, and I was excited. Amravati was a much larger city than Buldhana. It's not possible to cover the whole city with a bicycle. One could cover the entire Buldhana in 3 to 4hrs on cycle. Amravati was a perfect place for me to explore and learn new things. My mother sobbed as I prepared to leave for Amravati.

When I first arrived in the city, I had 1500rs and a bag containing some clothes and utensils, one stainless steel plate, one glass, and one spoon. With each of my new steps, that plate and the glass made noise. I was in an unknown city. I didn't know anyone there. I had to find a room before the evening, or else I'd have to sleep at the bus stop. After a whole day's search, I finally found the cheapest room for myself. The room rent was 1200rs per month. The room was on the first floor. It was actually a storehouse, and I felt lonely in that small room.

Just yesterday, I was in my hometown, with my family, and now I was sleeping all alone in an unknown city & in a strange room. I came out of the room and looked at the stars. That view was comforting.

I was fortunate that most of my tuition classmates from 12th had taken admission in various colleges of Amravati. There was a total of seven engineering colleges in Amravati.

In just one day, I found a roommate named Mangesh. He was also from Buldhana. And the rent was divided, 600rs per head (Me & Mangesh).

We quickly became a group of Buldhana friends. Prakhar, Kishore, Sameer, Aadarsh, Mangesh & Me. Apart from myself, everyone else came from a wealthy family. Sameer, Aadarsh, Mangesh and me were in the same college, i.e., MIT-Prestige engineering college. Prakhar and Kishore were in Rising Star engineering College.

We all became very close friends in a matter of days. Mangesh was a typical padhaku (studious). He used to avoid the rest of us and study in the room. All others were very fun-loving. They were not focused on studying, and they had no intention of passing and completing BTech. They were all too careless. I wasn't sure which category I belonged to. I wanted to pass the 1st semester, as well as I wanted to enjoy life. Apart from Aadarsh, I discovered that they all smoke and drink. Aadarsh used to drink 'Maaza' instead of alcohol at parties. I had always avoided alcohol and cigarettes all my life, so I used to go to my room during their party time. I always avoided all the parties and stayed away from all the addiction. My mind knew that being with Mangesh and studying would be more beneficial than staying with the rest of them. Mangesh had joined the private coaching classes for tough subjects in Semester 1, which were M1 (Mathematics 1), Mechanics, and ED (Engineering Drawing). I didn't have the funds to pay for any private coaching, so I joined none. Mangesh tried to convince me multiple times that the coaching classes were necessary if I wanted to complete the semester. I told him directly that I didn't have the money to pay for tuition. After hearing that, he just laughed for a minute. I felt a little embarrassed, but I wanted to know the reason behind his laugh. Nah, he was not that mean to look down on me. It was something else.

Mangesh: I can afford to pay for those classes, but I still don't. Because, as you can see, each batch has more than 150 students, and they run 2 to 3 batches. It makes no difference if one person does not pay. They already make lakhs of rupees.

Me: But how do they allow you to sit in class?

Mangesh: It's very simple; I told them I am very poor, and my father is a farmer. I even look like poor. Ha.

Mangesh's personality was fragile, and on top of that, he had a very dark complexion. He was short, probably about 4.9 or 5 feet tall. Mangesh had pimples all over his face. His face skin was damaged and scarred because of bursting those pimples. That suits his lie of being a farmer's son and going to the farm on all sunny days to have that dark skin.

Even though his suggestion was sound and practical for my current situation, my heart was saying no. I believe I already had a good experience with taking something for free in 12th grade. Instead of joining tuitions, I decided to refer to his notes. There was an unspoken competition between me and Mangesh. Whenever I used to sleep, he used to get the inspiration to study and vice versa. He wasn't very helpful in explaining the concepts to me, but he gave me the overview and allowed me to use all his tuition material.

In just a few days, we were over with our first semester, and the result was out.

Mangesh received 75%, while I got 60.5%.

The rest of my group, i.e., Prakhar, Kishore, Sameer, and Aadarsh, failed. Most of them had kt's (backlogs) in all subjects.

I was happy with my 60.5% because I didn't even have a single kt, although I spent most of the time with my bois. I told Mangesh to not talk about his percentage at my home.

"I am going to tell them that you got 65% because if I tell them you got a 75%, then my parents will think I am roaming and not paying attention to my studies while you study. You must do this for me because we are roommates", I tried to convince Mangesh.

Unfortunately, Mangesh didn't agree. He called my house and told them that he got 75%.

As I expected, I got scoldings. My mother reacted exactly the same as I thought. She was like, Mangesh studies all day, and you roam in the city. By the way, It was the bitter truth. Mangesh used to study the whole day. I could never do that even if I wanted to. I promised my mother that I would get a 75% in the next semester. Although I promised that, I had no plan to achieve it. I persuaded myself that I would study like Mangesh and won't go out with my boys. I also told Mangesh to help me so that I can get a percentage like him in the next sem.

The Second Semester started. That charm of studying every day like Mangesh lasted for a week, and then I came back to normal. I started spending more time with Sameer, Kishore, Prakhar and Aadarsh. There was a famous Chai-Wala named Laddus. Almost everybody in Farshi stop used to go there to have the tea. Most of the crowd in the area were engineering students, just like us. Having Chai and cigarettes at Laddus was like a custom there. It was always crowded, even if you go in the night, and one would hear conversations like kts, and how Mechanics and M1, M2, M3 are the toughest subjects, bunks, backbiting of teachers, and HOD's. I even saw people who were almost uncles talking about kts while smoking and drinking tea. They were the super seniors doing engineering for the last ten years but couldn't finish it because of backlogs (kts). Apart from Aadarsh, Mangesh & me, everyone else in the group became accustomed to having cigarettes & Chai every day at Laddus. In contrast, Aadarsh & I were happy with just tea.

Mangesh hardly came with us to Laddus.

Sameer & I used to go to Kathora square at Kishore's place. Kishore's place, aka Kishore and Prakhar's room, was well-known for parties. Kathora chowk was very far from the Farshi stop where we (Mangesh, Sameer, Aadarsh & I) lived. It was 7km, but that was a long-distance for us as we came from a small city.

Before taking admission to college, I considered bringing my cycle to Amravati, but after visiting the college, I dropped that idea. Otherwise, I would become the only person who uses a cycle in the entire college. I didn't want that much attention. It was an era of Bullet, ZMR and Pulsar 220. But Sameer and Kishore had splendor, and we were happy with that as we all used those two vehicles. It's better to have a splendor than walking or having a cycle. I used to go to college on Sameer's bike. Sameer was irregular so I became irregular as well. Our college MIT-Prestige Institute was 8km from the Farshi stop, so going there by walk was stupidity. The only other option was to walk until the Dastur Nagar stop, then take a 6 sitter for 7rs, exit just before the Badnera railway crossing, and walk another 2km. Trust me I have done that the first week of college. It was hectic.

You must wait until the six sitter is full because the driver will not start until then. It can take up to an hour at times. There is no other way to go to college unless you have your own vehicle. I preferred staying with Sameer and having fun rather than going to college regularly in that temperature. Yeah, Amravati was very hot, and as we all came from Buldhana, a hill station, it felt twice as hot. In that heat, walking 2km from Badnera railway crossing to college feels like you are actually in hell.

On one fine evening in winter, Sameer came to my room and told me that we had to go right now. We're going to the Chanakya Hotel for dinner. "I don't have money for eating in restaurants, so you go without me", I said. "You don't have to worry about that, even if I don't have the money. But Kishore is there, right? Whenever we all go out, and if Kishore is there at the party, he pays for everyone by default. You don't know the custom. Now don't say no and get ready. We are getting late", Sameer said. I didn't know how to respond to that, but I realised Sameer was serious. I remembered my own rule about not accepting anything for free from anyone because it never ends well, but Sameer was adamant, and he insisted so much that I had to go to the party.

Chanakya hotel Amravati was far away from the city. It took us nearly an hour to get there by bike. Kishore and Prakhar were already present and waiting for us.

This was my first time visiting any restaurant in Amravati city. Kishore gave me a thorough tour of the hotel and explained how good it was. We all moved to this city at the same time, but Kishore knew almost everything in Amravati. He knew every part of the city. What is famous for what, all the roads and shortcuts.

"Chanakya is famous for non-veg", Kishore said.

"I don't eat non-veg", I said. They all ordered non-veg, while I ordered veg food.

"You know what, you are in Chanakya, and you are eating veg. You are missing the point", Prakhar Said.

We all enjoyed the food and listened to Kishore's nonstop dirty jokes. I believe he will never run out of funny things to tell. We also enjoyed embarrassing moments from Prakhar's school life. My stomach was aching from laughing so much. As Sameer said earlier, Kishore paid the bill for everyone.

Just outside the hotel was a Pan Shop. We all ate "Maghai Paan", which was popular in Amravati. Later everyone smoked apart from me.

Then we started heading towards home.

The weather suddenly turned cold, and Prakhar said, "I'm feeling a little off". So, I told him to take the back seat, and I will drive. Sameer and Kishore were riding the other motorcycle.

Because the hotel was located outside of town, there was almost no one on the roads. They were completely empty. We were riding through the jungle, with lots of trees on both sides. Except for me, they were all wearing jackets. The bike's speed was 90-100. The cold breeze was hitting me hard. Sprinkling rain started within the next few minutes. I was still enjoying the ride.

Prakhar, who was sitting behind me, was shaking like anything because of the cold.

Even in that weather, Prakhar was able to light a cigarette.

"Have a puff; you will feel better", he said loudly so that I could hear him. He held the cigarette in front of my face.

I took the first cush of the cigarette while riding the bike.

That was my first cigarette puff ever.

It felt good.

Usually, people struggle when they smoke a cigarette for the first time. But I felt warm; I felt good. After that, we shared that cigarette equally. It was Gudang garam, so it lasted for our entire journey. I will never forget the first cigarette that I had in my life. I smoked it from Prakhar's hands as I was riding the bike.

After that day, Kishore and Prakhar started inviting me to every party at Kathora sq. I started spending more time with them.

Sameer used to come along with me to every party.

I started smoking and enjoyed it.

Soon I began eating egg and then chicken as well. I started taking things lightly and having fun in life.

I felt terrible the first time I ate non-veg because I was eating an innocent being for the sake of my taste.

I didn't sleep that night.

I was visualizing the whole picture, how they cut the meat & all.

But with time, that guilt faded away & within a few days, it was long gone.

I became hardcore non-vegetarian. Egg curry and chicken curry became my favourite dishes. I even started drinking. At a few parties, I drank too much and vomited. After that, I realised that I didn't enjoy losing my sanity & getting too drunk. I didn't like that feeling when you drink too much and have to vomit. Even the next day, you feel drowsy and dull.

After a few such experiments, I realised what I like and enjoy. I realised that I like to be in control, and too much alcohol takes that away from me. So, at each party, I started taking only 30ml, and that was it. In that way, I maintained my sanity and enjoyed the party as well.

I sometimes wondered why these people loved me that much. I didn't have any money to spend on them. But they never disrespected me, always took me to every party. I guess money and status don't matter that much in true friendship.

The way I was getting close to the gang, Mangesh became distant from me. He reduced talking with me. You can't be in both groups at the same time, I guess. Mangesh started spending more of his time with Pintu. Pintu was another copy of Mangesh, a studious one.

Pintu used to live alone in a room. 600-700 rs didn't matter that much to him. He was rich.

Mangesh and Pintu started studying together. Mangesh used to go to his room for studies. As the exam date approached, Mangesh and Pintu began devoting more time to their studies. At the same time, the number of parties in Kathora Square grew.

Mangesh came to me one day and said coldly, "I am leaving this room from next month & shifting to Pintu's. He lives alone there, and he needs a partner."

"Well, what about me? What will happen to the room rent? I can't give full 1200rs per month", I said.

"That's your problem; I am not bound to live here with you." He replied. I couldn't believe he really said that.

I was not worried because Mangesh was leaving the room and going to live with Pintu, but I was worried about the room rent. I couldn't possibly give the whole room rent. I immediately needed a roommate.

There was only one place where I could meet students from all engineering colleges, "Food mess of Dastur Nagar". I was somehow the famous personality in a mess as the aunty (Owner of the mess) used to tease me with that lipstick liner. "Hmm...lipstick diste othanvar, konale bhetun aala". Although that was a simple ruse, people used to admire me there. Yeah, I had female friends from mess and college, but they all were just friends. I was the same naive boy I used to be from inside, but my physics had changed. Suddenly my height was 5 feet 9 inches (5'9), and my voice started sounding deeper and more meaningful. God had blessed me with good looks, but I didn't have any girlfriend like people used to think there. On a serious note, few even asked me how to persuade women; they were not kidding; I can attest to that. I just told them to look into the eyes and be confident.

I wondered how someone could have such a stellar reputation without ever doing anything.

I told everyone in the mess that I was looking for a roommate. The news spread like wildfire. The next day, I got a roommate named Hari. He & his previous roommate had a fight. It was a blessing in disguise for me.

I found a better room and shifted there with my new roommate Hari.

Finally, the exams were over, and the second-semester results were out. I failed in all four subjects, and so did all my friends. Mangesh got distinction (75%) again.

We later discovered that at least four of the eight subjects must be cleared to progress to the second year of engineering.

I was all clear in 1st semester, so I was safe. On the other hand, Kishore, Sameer, Aadarsh, and Prakhar were not so fortunate. They all failed to complete that condition. It was evident that they were not going to the second year. By looking at their state, I thanked God for my result. Even though I failed in the second semester, I was eligible to go to 2nd year of engineering, and I was very happy with that.

But then I remembered the promise I had made to my mother. "I will get 75% next semester". Leave about 75% like Mangesh; I didn't even pass this time. How could I tell this result to my mother now? I was worried.

Mangesh did not call my house this time to tell about the result. We had kept our parents in the dark about the fact that we were no longer roommates.

Mangesh was somehow showing sympathy to me. Perhaps because my result was so poor that I was nowhere near him competitively. After thinking for quite a while, I made a plan. I took Mangesh's mark sheet, scanned it and edited it. I replaced his name with mine, and boom, I got 75% too. I also warned him not to tell anyone at home. He nodded.

I called my mother. There was a pride in my voice. I told her that I got 75% and Mangesh got 74%. She believed that. Everybody believed that. There was no need for that fake mark sheet, but I still kept it as a backup. And with that, the first year of my engineering was officially over.

CHAPTER TWENTY-EIGHT

Color of Money

My mess owner was very moody & unpredictable. She must be ten years older than my mother. Every Sunday, she used to make Paneer & Shrikhand, which was so delicious that you could never get such a taste at any hotel in Amravati. The food mess had a huge impact on my life. You might be thinking of the phrase "Jaisa khaye Ann, waisa hoye Man", but no, it was not just about good vegetarian food. Mess gave me so much more than that. It gave me contacts; that's how I met my new roommate Hari. I also met my new bike partner, 'Aaryan', there. Aaryan was also in CSE department, and we were in the same class.

One fine Sunday, my friends (Sameer, Aadarsh & Kishore) went to E-Orbit to buy new clothes and watch a recently released Hollywood movie. Only Prakhar & I stayed back as neither of us had money. My monthly quota was about to come next week, and Prakhar's parents had already sent the new month's quota, but he had already spent it all on alcohol and cigarettes. Our pockets were not completely empty. I had 30rs & Prakhar had 44rs (Including our bank accounts which were at zero).

As it was Sunday & Prakhar was at Farshi stop, I took Prakhar to my food mess. It was the day of Paneer & Shrikhand. As we entered the mess, I told aunty (Mess Owner) that I would pay an extra amount at the end of the month as I brought my friend with me. She shrugged. Everything appeared to have fallen into place. We were served delicious food, and everyone was pleased. However, we were unaware that this was the calm before the storm. As we started eating, Aunty (Mess Owner) started her lecture, "Students bring their friends to mess, particularly on Sunday and then they don't pay a dime later. I am used to it & this mess is not just a mess; it's a Dharamshala."

We both burst out laughing and coughing after hearing that.

Aunties words were a two-edged sword, which made us laugh, cough and give heartache at the same time. Thankfully we had only taken a little on our plate for a start, which was about to finish. We couldn't eat more than that anymore.

Both of us stood and said, "We are full, aunty; the food was delicious."

On our way back home(room), Prakhar said, "I will never come to your mess again, never again in my life, even if I die with hunger", & and we laughed until our empty stomachs hurt.

We had nothing to do, so we slept in the afternoon. In the evening, I considered bringing my food to the room as a parcel so that we could share it.

Prakhar and I went to Mess again, but Prakhar didn't come inside this time. When I went inside, I got to know that the Mess had closed. Aunty had declared half day.

I told Prakhar that I was not in the mood to eat anything now until tomorrow. Prakhar said the same, and we both laughed.

I bought a cornetto chocolate cone with my last 30rs in the memory of my father and our last meeting.

Prakhar bought a choti gold (cigarette) packet at 40rs. He still had 4rs left. So, he took one more choti gold in that 4rs. Hats off to our intelligence. We could have eaten something in that money & that could have filled our stomachs, but no, we were not in the mood anymore. We went to the terrace and shared ice cream and cigarettes. The building had four floors, and we were on the terrace, i.e., on the 5th floor. There were very few tall buildings nearby. Industrialization had not happened yet in Amravati. Although it was 5th floor still it felt like we were on top of the world.

A terrace in the middle of a full moon night can be a magical place. That night, we talked about our dreams and our worries.

Prakhar's brother and Prakhar were poles apart. His brother had 85% in 10th, and he had 50%. He barely passed in 12th, while his brother had 190 out of 200 in CET & got admitted into autonomous engineering college, which was my dream a few years ago. His brother was always a topper. So, there were many expectations from Prakhar that he couldn't ever deliver. We discussed life without money & its true meaning. What's enough, and what else do we want apart from money? With each passing cigarette, we discussed our fears & dreams, and the weight on our hearts felt lighter than before.

All of our friends (Sameer, Kishore, and Aadarsh) returned at 1 a.m.

They were gushing about how good the movie was and how enjoyable their day had been.

But Prakhar and I knew we had a much better day than the rest of our friends.

CHAPTER TWENTY-NINE

Planning of an adolescent

Boys have abnormal psychology when it comes to college girls. Nobody likes the girls in their batch. They will favour either seniors or juniors. At last, they won't ever like the girls in their department or class. They will always feel there is more greenery in another department. Yes, there are exceptions to every theory, but I'm talking about the general mentality. CSE is famous for many things, but the most important thing is greenery. You might have heard good Hindi slogans for other branches like "Sabka baap Ek hai, mech hai mech hai", but they all come to the CSE department to see the greenery. And when nothing works, they all work in IT.

My batchmates and friends were waiting for juniors as the new year began. That craze lasted for a month and then faded out.

One evening, Sameer and I were out for a stroll, and we noticed a group of girls from our class eating ice cream at "farshi stop".

"I have a plan," Sameer said after seeing that group. At that moment, I knew that the plan would be very absurd & surreal.

The plan was like this: "We will take the cigarette from the nearest pan shop and then walk towards them in style while smoking. Then we will stand in one corner and smoke there. And after some time, one of us will speak with the girls. The conversation start would be. 'You girls are from MIT-Prestige college?' and according to their response, we will take it further from there."

I lit the classic mild in style, and then we walked towards them. As we reached one corner, we continued our fake conversation. But none of us was ready to start the conversation with the girls. After a few seconds, one of the girls in the group shouted. "Eww, they are smoking, and all the smoke is coming towards us." Another girl made a disgusting face and gave us a dirty look. And in the next second, the whole group stood up and disappeared in no time.

"Thank god we didn't start the conversation with them", Sameer said.

And we laughed until our stomachs ached.

When I arrived at college the next day, most of the girls in my class were giving me the same disgusting look that we got last night. Perhaps smoking was not as cool in Amravati as we thought. I'm not sure what Sameer thought when he made the plan yesterday. Did he think Amravati suddenly became New York? And who am I to question him as I agreed with the plan in the first place. I was talking to myself.

While I was going to the canteen, one of my classmates (a girl) came from the opposite side. When she was about to cross me, she literally changed the lane. It's just a coincidence, I told myself. But similar incidents happened with a couple of other girls in the next few weeks. I realised that these girls from my class won't ever talk with me. Is smoking really that bad?

I had missed practicals as I was not regular in college. Our class captain Disha was the perfect candidate to ask for the details. She was a prodigy and used to attend college regularly. Everybody knew that.

When I asked her about the copy,

I got this:

"Umm...there is nothing much in there; you could ask someone else".

"Yeah, there is nothing much in it; that's why you got distinction last Sem."

I wanted to say that. But I just smiled and left.

My mind was saying one thing to me, "This all happened because of the world-class planning of your dear friend Sameer."

But that couldn't stop us from smoking.

At the entry gate of the college, there used to be two security guards. I took them to the unofficial canteen outside of college and told Sameer to pay for their anda-poha. After that day, I started entering college on Aaryans splendor with a cigarette in my mouth. That entry was way cooler than students & their two 20s, bullets, and ZMR.

Aaryan became the new group member in our friend's circle. We were in the same class. He was the person who was ready to give his blood & sweat for friendship. All credit goes to the food mess; otherwise, we wouldn't have become best friends. Aaryan was the one who was taking real advantage of being in the computer science department. He had a way with women. He had many girlfriends. Aaryan's roommate was ultra-rich. He had two bikes, One ZMR & One Bullet. Aaryan used to ride one of those, and I used to ride his bike splendor. In the entire Btech years, his splendor was parked more in front of my room than his flat. It was officially mine, but he was the one who paid for petrol. We had an unofficial udhaar account.

At that time, I didn't know that I would settle that account after completing BTech & not before that.

I was short of cash as I was not regularly getting money from my home. And on top of that, my expenditure had increased as compared to the previous year because of an additional burden of cigarettes. I was not in the mood to distribute newspaper as that small amount couldn't satisfy my increased needs. I had become extremely lazy by staying with my lazy friends. I wanted to create something that would have lot of demand. And the target audience was my fellow Btech batchmates.

What does a BTech student really want? One day, I asked that question to Sameer.

His answer was something like this.

1. I want a pulsar 220
2. CSE departments beauty as my girlfriend
3. Lot of cash

4. And all the question papers for 1st & 2nd Sem so that I won't fail again in my 1st year of Btech

His words rang a bell in my mind, and I ran toward my room. Sameer had no idea what was going on, he was stunned. Exams for the third semester were about to begin. My goal was to predict a question paper for at least one subject. Yeah, plain stupid, I know. The most feared subjects in the 3rd Sem were M3 (Mathematics III) & EDC (Electronic devices & circuits). I was good at math, so I was not worried about M3. But no one can predict M3 as it's not a theoretical subject. My target audience (consumers) was so dumb that even if you gave them the same type of example, they couldn't solve it if the values were changed. So, I knew I couldn't touch M3.

I saw the old question papers of EDC; they were all filled up with theory questions. Fortunately, I was present in college when the teacher gave IMP for EDC. I went to a nearby cyber-café, copied all those IMP questions, and added the questions that were recently asked in the last three years and voilà, my question paper was ready.

I knew that at least 50% to 60% of questions would come from my custom-made paper because the questions actually covered 40% of the syllabus, and the probability of coming two more questions from the IMP was high. I took a print of that money-making question paper. I knew I had done a good job, although my conscience was saying it wasn't right.

When there were only two days left to EDC paper, I knew it was time to sell my fantastic product. Panic & desperation has their way of creating demand for everything. Also, students won't complain about me to anyone when the toughest subject exam is on their head, and I am providing all the help at a minimal cost.

"I am offering the question paper at 400rs with the guarantee of 60% questions. And if that doesn't happen, I will return the money", I assured them.

Some of the roommates argued that only one of them would buy the question paper, on which I told them, "I got the paper from some confidential authorities, and there is a target that I have to achieve. I am only getting some amount as my commission. So, either both of you take the paper or don't take it at all." And they all just agreed in every room.

I only reached out to mediocre students I knew personally. I avoided students who had 60% & above in the last Sem. Most of my target students were from my food mess. I also warned them that don't forward this to anyone else and be quiet about it. If something goes wrong, then we all have to bear the consequences. That sentence made my question paper look more legit.

I earned 11200rs in two days. It was a large sum for me. I sold the question paper to 28 students. I made a list of those 28 names. 11200rs means I didn't have to worry about anything for the next five months. My monthly expenditure was something like this

1. 750rs Room rent
2. 1200rs Food mess
3. 200 to 300rs on Cigarettes

"I was not a fan of alcohol. I think it is overpriced for its bitter taste. In my opinion, the best time to have drinks is when you are tired from descending the mountains, or you are in a freezing place or when it's raining outside or if you are with your best friends exploring new places.

For me, 30ml is fine (even if it's free of cost) as I like to be in control, and I don't enjoy losing sanity, unlike others. I also believe in expensive single malt whiskies. But this is definitely not the time to give it a try".

I didn't spend a single penny from the amount that day. Because if 60% of questions didn't come from my paper in tomorrow's exam, then I will have to return the whole amount to all my 28 fellas as I had assured. I don't deviate from my promises.

I went to the exam hall with 100% confidence the next day. Somewhere in my mind, I was considering myself a question setter as well.

When the real question paper came in my hand, I was delighted.

70% of the questions were from my question paper. It was my day.

CHAPTER THIRTY

Departments Beauty

The third-semester results were out. I had only cleared two subjects, M3 & EDC. All the remaining subjects were backlogs. I think I gave all my efforts to predicting the EDC question paper and ignored the rest. Mangesh got 80% in the 3rd sem. He was now beyond my reach & I couldn't even think about competing with him anymore.

For the rest of my bois, it was 1st Sem (because of the year down). They never cared much about exams & results. I didn't have the strength to lie about my marks this semester, so I told the truth at home. (Although I kept my old lie of distinction in 2nd Sem intact)

My bois were hanging out with junior girls (as a friend, lol) because they were no longer juniors and had become batchmates.

In each department, there is at least one extremely beautiful girl. And the whole department knows her name.

In the new batch (1st year), it was "Anisha Grewal". Her fame as a 'Marvellous beauty of the CSE department' spread like wildfire.

My overjoyed batchmates had shown me her one day.

She really was above the line.

As my fourth semester began, I was on the lookout for major setbacks. I wanted to start from the basics and then build on top of that.

The minimum criteria for a student to go to the 3rd Year of BTech were simple,

1. The first year should be all clear. (All subjects from 1st & 2nd Sem)

2. At least two subjects from the second year should be clear.

And that was my primary goal to meet the bare minimum of requirements in order to progress to 3rd year.

I was very bad at programming, which is the core of CSE. I had a backlog subject 'Computer programming' from 2nd Sem (1st year). As I had earned enough money by selling EDC question paper last Sem, I knew I could join the private coaching class for 'C Programming', which would help build my logic and general knowledge about programming.

I didn't want to go to a private coaching class as a poor student who needed concession. So, I tried to disguise myself as an upper-middle-class student. I did some shopping for the first time in the last one & half years.

I bought a black jacket at 600rs and one full-sleeved round neck light-grey t-shirt at 400. I also borrowed Sameer's red colour full sleeves t-shirt and his spykar jeans. And I already had Aaryan's splendor.

The next day, I went to Amravati's well-known coaching institute, CCIT. I joined the next upcoming batch. The fees were 1500rs which I paid in full on the 3rd day, as the teacher was very knowledgeable. Just two lectures were more than enough to create interest in the language for someone like me who hated programming. The class was packed with first-year students. Students usually prefer to clear the subject in their regular Sem and don't like to pile up.

I promised myself that I would not miss a single class.

The next day, I missed it as I had to rush to the hospital for my roommate Hari. He felt like he had a heart attack.

How could someone get a heart attack in their 20s, I was wondering. The doc cleared our doubts. It was GERD and not a heart attack. We were both relieved when we heard that. When I arrived at CCIT the next day, I noticed a known face while entering the class. She was the department's beauty, CSE diva "Anisha

Grewal".

I needed notes from yesterday's lecture, and she would be a good candidate, I told myself.

Nah, I didn't forget the last incident with my class captain. And I like to learn from my mistake.

"But just because someone turned you down doesn't mean the rest of the world will, " I reassured myself.

Some people like to help others, and some don't. We just have to move on and try again. And the objective to request notes for yesterday's lecture was genuine. I didn't even think about making the department's beauty as my GF or anything (like 80% of my department's male students). It was just more fun to take notes from her than anyone else.

After the class, I walked towards her when everybody was going towards their vehicle and about to leave. I looked into her eyes & said,

"Hi... (paused for 2 seconds). Did you attend yesterday's class?

'Yeah', she said and nodded as well.

I was absent yesterday. Can I borrow your register? I will bring it back tomorrow, I promise.

She took a long pause, which created a void in the conversation and made it awkward.

She then opened her backpack and handed me the register.

I took it and smiled as I said, "Thank you."

Her handwriting was excellent, even better than mine.

As promised, I returned it the next day.

A few days went like this; I was attending the tuition regularly. One day after the tuition, I went to panshop next to the parking area. I bought a cigarette and lit it.

I was wearing my new full sleeves grey t-shirt and Sameer's Spykar jeans.

It was a beautiful evening; the sun was about to set.

I looked towards the majestic saffron sky & took one more cush from the cigarette.

While I was lost in the stunning view of the sky,

I heard a familiar voice.

'Hi.................'

It was Anisha, the department's beauty.

I looked towards her in disbelief and took another cush from the cigarette.

While blowing out that inhaled smoke, I said, 'Hello, Anisha'.

"Could you help me with the scooty? I couldn't take it out", She said while motioning with her hand in the direction of her vehicle.

'Yeah', I replied.

We walked towards her scooty. Lot of boys and girls from the class were looking at us.

It was parked in the middle of the queue & there were at least 15 two-wheelers on both sides of her scooty.

And most of them were parked so close to each other that it would be difficult for anyone to take their vehicle out.

There was little space after the 5th bike on the left side of her scooty. I took one more cush from the cigarette before dropping it deftly, and then I crushed the stub with my feet.

I started moving the bikes; I had to move five bikes to clear the space for her scooty.

She sat on her scooty and pressed the self-start.

Then she looked at me and said coldly, 'What's your name?'

"I am Vijay", I said.

'Thank you so much, Vijay', she said, blushing. Her face turned red, and her hair was blowing on her face. She looked more stunning on that lovely evening.

The next day in the class, my eyes were searching for her. I found her sitting on the 4th row on the left side (girls' side). I was in the 7th row. The class was going on, and at one instance, she caught me staring at her. She gave a modest smile, and I smiled back naturally. I tried to concentrate on the lecture after that & didn't look again at the girls' section.

After the class, Anisha & one more girl walked toward me.

'Hi, umm.. we both are going to CCD; would you like to join us? She asked.

I agreed and started the splendor with a kick. This was my first time going to CCD. I saw the name cappuccino on the menu, which sounded cool, so I ordered that. They both ordered cold coffee. When the cappuccino arrived, the guy kept the sugar packet beside the coffee. I was accustomed to drinking tea and cigarette at the roadside shops. But I played the act. I opened one sugar packet delicately, put it in the coffee and stirred.

'So, you don't like much sugar in your coffee', her friend said.

'Yeah, the originality of coffee will get lost if you use too much sugar', I said.

'You are from which college?' Anisha's friend asked again.

The same as Anisha's. I wanted to say that, but I restrained myself.

'I am from MIT-Prestige college', I said.

'Old or new?'

'Old'. I replied

'I am from MIT-Prestige as well', Anisha said.

'She means we all are from MIT-Prestige'. Her friend said while giving her an odd look.

'So, how's your 1st year going? Being in a new college and all', her friend asked again.

'I am in 2nd year. I joined C Programming class because it's a backlog from 2nd Sem', I said.

'OH, you are our senior then', Anisha said.

Technically, yes,' I replied.

As the conversation was getting boring, I took the initiative and played the 'Never have I ever' game with them. And all the things from crushes to alcohol started coming out from those innocent faces.

Then I asked them simple questions and predicted a few things from their past.

I was not entirely correct while predicting, but most of the things were right like

1. They have known each other for the last one year and not before that.

2. Anisha liked Hollywood movies while her friend liked Bollywood more.

The more her friend laughed & got entertained, the more she (Anisha) started giving me that spooky look filled with infatuation. Anisha became uneasy every time her friend giggled and touched me.

Anisha's friend insisted and paid the bill in the end.

After that day, Anisha and I became close friends and began hanging out together.

On one fine morning, when I was still sleeping, my phone rang. It was Anisha.

"Hi, my scooty has some problem. Can I come with you to college?" She asked.

'Yeah, of course. I spoke.

It was eight o clock in the morning when her call awakened me. I washed my college uniform and cleaned my shoes. Our college had a dress code that made us look like we were still in primary school. Every year had its own dress code except final year. Those guys could wear whatever they wanted. One can easily identify who is in which year.

As I didn't have much time for the clothes to get soaked, I ironed them. I took a shower and got ready. I was finally going to college after a long time. The last time I was this UpToDate was one and a half years ago, during the first week of my BTech. The security guards waved and smiled as I entered through the college gate. They were probably wondering, "Where is the cigarette in his mouth?" "How come he is wearing a clean shirt?" or "How come this guy has a beautiful girl sitting behind him instead of his friend Aaryan?"

All the nerds in the parking area were looking at me with their awful faces. Yeah, only nerds attend college and are present on time.

We entered our CSE department together.

I deliberately went with her until she entered her class. Before going inside, she waved. My juniors, the first-year boys, looked at me as if I had stolen Kohinoor from them. Then I went to the third floor and went into my class. For the first time in the last one and half years, college felt better.

In the recess, as I walked towards the canteen, two girls from my class waved at me. I smiled back.

I ordered my food and sat alone in a corner. While I was eating, the class captain came in and said, 'Nice to see you in college after such a long time,' and then left. She was the same girl who had refused to give her notes. These girls used to cross lanes and avoid me at all costs; now, they were waving at me. It was the strange day in college.

A few days went like this. Anisha & I saw a couple of Hollywood movies together at Rajesh (Rajesh Big Cinema) & E-Orbit. I was living a perfect but delusional life.

Every time I met Anisha, it made a hole in my pocket.

Anisha wanted to become a model. She desired fame & money in her life. One day when I went to pick her up in the neighbourhood, she was roaming with someone.

"He is Agneya. He is my ex", she said casually.

I had never seen that much frankness before in my life.

She was the only child of her parents & grew up in a wealthy family. She always got what she wanted. She had not seen the harsh realities of this world, and I was glad about that.

But I didn't like the way she was hanging out with her ex. I was not that frank.

We both liked watching Hollywood movies. A multiplex is a magical place to visit on sunny afternoons. Amravati's summer afternoon temperatures range from 45° to 50° Celsius. Going to a dark place with a temperature of 20° C maintained by air conditioners is bliss in summer.

On one such afternoon, while watching a movie, she (Anisha) squeezed my hand tightly. Was it because of the cold or something else? I was not sure. She had never done that before. I must agree, I felt good.

Then she looked directly into my eyes and asked, "You haven't been with many girls, have you?"

"Not in Amravati", I said mischievously.

'And you have never watched a movie with another girl apart from me?'

"No, dear", I said.

Your hands are so warm, she said.

I stared at her lovely face and said nothing.

She then moved closer to me. I wrapped her in my arms. She moved her head closer to mine, looked in my eyes, and kissed me the next second.

It was the first time a girl had ever kissed me.

It's something you never forget.

We roamed around the city in the evening. We ate at Raghuvir Rajapeth. Anisha's parents had gone out of town, so she didn't worry about getting home on time. We went to 'Maltekdi', a famous spot for couples in Amravati.

'Have you ever travelled outside of India?' she asked.

No. 'I've never been anywhere, really,' I said.

She told me about all the places she'd visited. She described the countries she had visited in Europe. She tried her best to explain to me how beautiful those countries were.

Maltekdi was the highest point in Amravati. I was looking at the whole city while holding hands with the department's beauty.

"Life is so unpredictable", I was telling myself.

'What are you thinking? She asked. Her question brought me back to reality from the loop of my thoughts.

'Nothing,' I replied.

No. You have to tell me.

'Do you really wanna know the truth, Anisha'.

'YYYeahhaaa', she asked with a somewhat cautious tone.

'What you are seeing right now is a man in borrowed clothes. I can't even afford the monthly expenses sometimes.'

'What about that black jacket of yours? Is it yours?', She asked

'Yeah, that's mine.'

"And How about your bike? Isn't it yours or your father's?'

'No, I borrowed that as well.'

'But it's always with you.' 'How is that even possible?'

'My friend's roommate has two bikes, ZMR & Bullet. So they both ride one of those. He no longer requires his splendour, so he gave it to me.

He also put the petrol in it every week so that I can use it.'

'Of-course', She said.

And how you manage all the bills of movie tickets in the theatre and everything. I don't reckon I ever paid anywhere.

'Well, I sold a question paper for one of the toughest subjects in the third semester'.

'You mean you leaked the question paper before the actual exam date and sold it to earn money?' She asked in disbelief.

'Yeah & I earned 10200rs..........nooooooooo..... actually 11200rs with that ', I said.

'My goodness,' She said and started laughing.

She continuously laughed for a minute and then spoke while pushing me impishly, 'Vijayyyyyy......'.

We both burst out laughing.

'I thought I met an honest man, but youuuuuuuuuuu'. She said mischievously.

I had told her the truth.

But it was all a ruse for her.

We lost track of time. It was almost midnight. Every hour felt like a minute, and before we knew it was already 12.15 AM.

We started heading towards her home.

Anisha's friend, who had come for a sleepover, was waiting for her at her house.

We reached in front of her house in no time.

She opened the huge compound door while I parked the splendor outside.

We entered the compound. There was a beautiful lawn on both sides.

'Well, I had a wonderful day Vijay', She said.

'So did I, Anisha'.

The compound walls were 7 feet high, but still, she looked both ways to make sure no one was watching us.

She came closer to me. She was about to kiss me on the lips, but I moved my head, and she kissed me on my cheek instead.

'You are welcome to come inside. My parents are not home.'

'I know'

'... I should be going. We will meet again, I promised calmly.

She nodded.

'Good night then, Vijay', She said.

'Good night Anisha'.

How could I let her fall into the world of poverty and pain?

How could I bring her to misery?

If I truly cared for her, then the kindest thing I could do was to walk away.

I turned back and looked at her for one more time.

She was looking stunning.

Then I continued walking in the darkness to reach the bike.

I kick-started the splendor and started heading toward my room. While crossing the flyover, I thought about all the moments I had spent since morning, watching the movie, eating at raghuvir, and then spending time at Maltekdi.

All the visuals of those moments were flashing in front of my eyes.

I was watching the highlight of my life.

There was nobody around, nothing. No other car, just me and the splendor.

Before I could realise it, I was in my room.

As I was about to sleep, my phone rang. It was Anisha.

Me: Hi

Anisha: Can you come outside of your room?

Me: Now?

Anisha: Yeah, just come outside. Please.

I went outside, and I saw her standing in front of the gate. I was trying to understand the situation.

Before I could ask her anything, she spoke, "I just couldn't sleep. I was thinking about you."

'Okay, but you could have waited until morning; it's not wise to travel alone at night. What were you thinking?' I asked.

'I think I might have given you the wrong impression; I usually don't travel at such hour.

Also, I am not looking for a relationship. I have learned that from my last bf. My goal in life is simple. Live free and enjoy life.

I want to do modelling; I will be a star one day. She was gasping while saying all that.

'I know you will be a star one day. But what is it you want from me that you have to come here at this hour?'

'I like your company'. She said.

'Even I like spending time with you.' I said.

'Can you come with me to my house? I will make you a coffee and Maggie', she said with a trembling voice.

The intensity with which the events were unfolding, I could not grasp what was going on.

I just looked in the direction of the road for a few seconds.

I was not able to see anything after the turn.

The road was as unpredictable as my next move.

Finally, I sat behind her on the scooty.

She was talking all the way up to her house. But I don't remember a word of it apart from the line, 'I am not looking for a relationship'. We stopped near the railway station. Had Coca-Cola and smoked there.

All the roads were empty as people were not crazy enough to drive in the middle of the night.

Her friend Aditi (who had come for a sleepover) waved at me from the 2nd-floor window when we entered inside the compound.

As promised, Anisha made me the coffee and Maggie.

It was the best coffee-maggie combination I ever had.

I loved it.

I spent the night with her.

Anisha was the first woman that ever loved me.

I couldn't wait to see her again. We saw each other every evening.

Our meeting place was Maltekdi. Each visit seemed special and new.

One day, When I went to pick her up, I saw her with her ex. His hands were wrapped around her neck. I stopped the splendor and waited for them to see me. After a few seconds, she saw me and waved. I didn't wave back; I started the bike and left.

I didn't say anything to her regarding that in our next meeting, but she seemed distant this time. I started avoiding meeting her at CCD and multiplexes as my savings was almost over. I couldn't afford her anymore. But she never took the initiative to pay at any place ever. Maybe she didn't realise that there could be a case that I couldn't have any money. And with time, the distance between us grew.

In a few months, we almost stopped talking with each other.

After a very long time, I got a message from her as it was my birthday. "Happy Birthday Vijay. It was nice to meet you".

And that was it.

I was not in the right mind. I didn't know why I was so hurt, but I was. I was feeling completely hopeless. Maybe I was depressed. Was it because of Anisha? I don't know because she had clarified from the start that she didn't want any relationship. What about what I wanted? I didn't really know. I am not sure that I wished for a long-term relationship either. Or maybe I wanted a long-term relationship.

The truth was simple, 'I was in pain, and I didn't know what I wanted from my life.'

One day, while I was sitting in the classroom minding my own business, a teacher called my name and blamed me for laughing. 'I was not laughing, I said laughingly. And the entire class laughed. He got annoyed and told me to leave the class, which I gladly did. After a few days, he again told me to leave when I entered the class. This was the second time. I didn't understand the reason but left the class.

Everything was jumbling up in my head, Anisha Grewal, Cash crunch, every day's struggle, I was losing my mind.

I waited for the third time. And the third time came.

When he asked me to go out, I stood up, took my backpack and said firmly, 'You could never be a good teacher. You point out someone without any reason. The whole class was silent.

I continued, "I don't really need you to teach me the subject. You are not that good anyway." He made a face like he didn't believe what had just happened.

The whole class was like, 'Wooooooooooooooooooooooooh'.

And it satisfied my foolish ego.

He complained about me to HOD. And HOD Sir asked me to come to his cabin. Only one week was left for the college, and I was thinking, 'Why did I have to make this mess? I could have tolerated him for one more week. Or I just had to be absent for one more week. I never attended college regularly anyway. It was no big deal. Why didn't I back off?'

But my other stubborn mind was saying, 'I did the right thing. It's a greater sin to suffer the injustice.'

I had done whatever has to be done and I was ready to bear the consequences.

HOD Sir told me to bring my parents, to which I said, "I won't bring my parents because I am not wrong. Chopda Sir is the one who made a mistake by throwing me out three times from the class without any reason". I was firm and obstinate.

Somehow the HOD Sir understood me and told me to go and sit in the class. It was just sheer luck that the department's HOD was the best HOD in the whole college, and he didn't take any action against me.

Exams for my 2nd-semester backlog subjects had started. Fourth semester exams (my regular sem) were about to begin next week. I even had the backlogs from the third semester as I had cleared only M3 and EDC in 3rd sem.

I was prepared for 2nd-semester backlogs. I solved them with full enthusiasm.

The first paper for the fourth semester was ALP (Assembly Language programming).

I was prepared for ALP, as I liked that subject. But I was zero % ready for other subjects. I was not even prepared for my 3rd-semester backlogs.

I had one week in my hand, which was more than enough to prepare for a few subjects, but I didn't feel like studying anymore. So, I did nothing that week.

The condition for going to 3rd year was simple. 1st year should be all clear and two subjects from 2nd year. I had already cleared two subjects from the 3rd Sem, and my papers for the 2nd Sem (1st year) went well. So, my goal was already achieved. And hence I cared nothing.

My childhood friend Sarvesh was in Mumbai at that time.

I called him and said, "My fourth sem exams are beginning tomorrow. ALP is the 1st paper, and I am prepared for it. I am not prepared for any other subject. I couldn't write a single word in any other paper (apart from ALP). So, after tomorrow's paper, I will come to Mumbai. I will stay at your place for a few days. And I'll take care of the rest of the subjects the following semester. I don't want to worry about them right now. I will clear them all in next semester."

And he understood that. No questions asked; that's the beauty of an old friend.

I didn't even have the money to book a tatkal ticket for the journey, so he told me he would do it for me.

The next day, as I was writing the paper for ALP at 10 AM, Sarvesh was trying to book a tatkal ticket for that same night. After the exam, I learned that he couldn't as all the seats were sold out in the very first minute.

So, he transferred me 500rs. I went to the railway station and bought the waiting ticket in sleeper class at 410rs. At least I could get into the sleeper compartment. When I got ready to start the journey, I couldn't find that ticket. I had lost it somewhere. I looked everywhere in my room but couldn't find it. I didn't have any confirmed PNR, as it was a waiting (WL) ticket.

I called Sarvesh again, and he transferred me 200rs. I took that out from ATM, went to the railway station, and bought a general ticket at 170rs.

I'm not too fond of the general compartment. But it was fate that I had to travel in that for the whole night.

I arrived Dadar station at 6.30 a.m. I didn't even have enough money to buy breakfast. My phone battery was about to run out. And my phone's balance was 1.5rs. I made that last call to Sarvesh and told him that I had reached the station and waiting at the entrance-exit gate.

It was my first-time visiting Mumbai. There was no way back as I had no money, including my bank accounts. I waited for him for the next 2hrs.

Sarvesh reached at 8.30.

I gave him my backpack to carry and told him to buy two cigarettes. We smoked at the station. This was the first time in my life that I was smoking with Sarvesh. I felt better seeing him smoked. We both were happy about our bad habits.

"At least we could give company to each other," I said, and we both laughed.

Then we started heading towards Kurla, where his room was.

I stayed in Mumbai for many days. While I was roaming in locals with Sarvesh and seeing different parts of the city, my classmates were giving exams for 4th sem subjects.

I saw many places in Mumbai, including the Gateway of India.

I loved sitting at the marine drive.

The travelling was free for us. We never bought the ticket for local. We never thought about getting caught, and we never feared any TC. It was just dumb luck that nobody caught us ever, not even once.

Sarvesh didn't have any cook. He used to cook on his own. We made a couple of recipes like Poha, Egg Maggie, Egg Poha, Chicken fry, Tandoori chicken, egg curry, and egg bhurji. I developed my own egg bhurji recipe, which was way better than the normal one. You just have to boil the eggs before making the bhurji.

In Mumbai, it was raining every single day. We never cared about it. We loved wandering in the rain.

I had my first Gin in Mumbai. It was raining heavily that day, and we had two drinks (30ml each) on the road while roaming in the night. Then we had the rest of the bottle in the room. We talked about all our childhood memories, our favourite adde (spots) in Buldhana and, of course, mountains & valleys.

These were the most thrilling and happiest days of my life. We roamed in the city without any shirt or t-shirt on when the rain was flooding the streets. You can feel the raindrops better when you are naked.

We drank and smoked until our stomachs hurt.

We stayed up all night playing video games (Contra and Mario) and smoking. We ate when we felt like it. Frequently visited marine drive & south Mumbai to see hot chicks.

Sarvesh gifted me a new red coloured t-shirt on my last day in Mumbai.

'I don't have anything to give you apart from a hug', I said.

'And that is more than enough, he replied.

"I will always remember these days", I said before bidding him goodbye.

CHAPTER THIRTY-ONE

Redemption

The result was out for the 4th sem. It was as expected. I could only clear one subject, ALP, as I was absent for all the remaining papers. The score was Zero in all of them. And I had Zero internal in TOC (Theory of Computation). As the HOD sir didn't take any action against me, this was the only thing chopda sir could do, and he did that. Although I was eligible to go to 3rd year, I knew I was standing on the verge of getting a year down. I realised that I won't make it to the final year (4th Year) if I couldn't act now. I had to take an exam for 12 subjects this semester, two subjects from the third semester, four subjects from the fourth semester, and the entire fifth semester (Five subjects from 5th Sem).

I didn't have any money left and had to wait on my family to send it. I had unpaid rent for the last two months (750 plus 750).

The owner aunty used to sit in front of the gate to catch me while going out and coming in. I used to avoid her at all costs. I was sure she would throw me out if I didn't pay this month. I knew that if I didn't take any steps now, I would soon reach the point of saturation, and from there, the comeback would be very difficult. It was time for me to get my life in order.

I received a call from an unknown number one evening. It was my dad.

I recognized his voice from the first word 'Hello'.

I had not spoken with him in a long time.

He asked me some basic questions like how's my health and how the college is going on. I answered all those questions politely.

There was some emptiness in our conversation, and we both could recognize that.

I wanted to ask him so many questions, but I didn't ask anything.

It was a one-way conversation. He asked the questions, and I replied.

I talked politely, but beneath that courtesy, there was a deep reservoir of feelings.

After a few days, I received another call from him. He asked me whether I needed money to buy a motorcycle.

"You can decide to buy any motorcycle you wish, and I will send you the required amount", He said.

That sentence gave me the semblance that he has enough money and is doing well in his life (at least in the perspective of money).

"I don't need the money for a bike, but you can start with a few thousand. That would help as I am in dirt debt and need money to eat."

I wanted to say that. I really wanted to say that, but I didn't.

I declined his offer for a new bike and said **I don't need anything**.

That night, I saw a dream; normally, I don't remember my dreams, but this one was vivid and colourful.

It was about my father. He was deep in the mountains, and the winter was coming. He could only come out from that place in summer when the snows would melt, and the passes would open.

He had no device, not even a watch. He was only aware of the year 2012, day unknown, month unknown. He had been travelling for a long time. It had been almost seven years, living from day to day, moving from place to place with no idea of where he was going.

He began his journey in search of an answer to the eternal question, "Who am I?" Just like his son. And one night, when he was sleeping at the top of the mountain & gazing at the stars, he remembered his family, his son.

He keeps the diary with him wherever he goes and writes in it just like his son.

He was writing something.

He was writing a letter to me.

Dear Son,

It's been a long time since I saw you. I wish I could have been there to teach you how to ride a bicycle. I wish I could have seen you when you fell from the cycle for the first time and stood again. I think about you all the time. It's not the conscious thought, really. I wish I could have been there to teach you a motorcycle. I wish I could have felt the wind with you when you put that 4th gear and gave full accelerator. When I was going through the peaks in the Himalayas, you were with me; when I went to Mount Kailash, you were with me; when I was taking a dip in the river Ganga, you were with me. I have started to think that this whole expedition was a mistake. You are someone who occupies my mind and heart in this unknown place where I am right now. I am here deep in the mountains, which are protected by heavy snow walls. I am living among these unusual people. They don't have any materialistic achievements. They are less concerned about worldly chores, but they are more peaceful at heart than our sophisticated people ever could be. I can't say I know where I am going and whether I will ever reach my destination in this life. I don't know if my bad deeds will get purified by visiting all these distant sacred places and rivers. For the world, we are miles apart, but you are closer to me than you think. I hope one day you will understand that the great distance between us couldn't fade the love I have for you. I wish I could convey more, but words have their own constraints.

With Love,

Your Father.

When I woke up, I checked the old mailbox hanging over at my landlord's gate. I didn't find any letter in that for me. It was just a dream. Very vivid but still just a dream.

I was the only link between my father and the rest of my family. No one was ready to talk with him yet. He must be very lonely and sad. You can be mad and resent someone for the rest of your life, but at some point in your life, you have to let it go. Life is too short to hold grudges and complaints. I never wanted to squander away this short span of life in resentment; I was trying to appreciate it.

I was very happy that my dad called me after all these years.

As I had declined to take any money from my father, I needed some immediate patch for my current situation. I borrowed 2k from Aaryan, paid the rent & bought Dwivedi's for a few subjects. Then, for the first time in two years, I went to the college library. I borrowed books from there and made notes as per the syllabus. I went to see Tayde, a college friend. He never had a backlog and was consistent in his result range of 60 to 70%. I didn't want to be a topper or have a distinction. I knew that was not realistic with these many backlogs. I just wanted to clear all the subjects and keep my average above 60% so that I could be eligible for the college campus. Tayde guided me well. I referred to his notes and made a xerox for myself.

I started visiting Tayde's place regularly. He was the only studious friend I had in my branch. I got some books and notes from him free of cost as they were the backlog subjects. He didn't need those anymore. Tayde also taught me a few chapters for my backlog subjects as he was good at them. Every subject usually had six chapters. I prepared four chapters for each subject except TOC. I prepared all six chapters for that subject as I had Zero internals.

I stopped smoking and avoided going to all parties. I always gave some reasons to Sameer when he used to ask me to go out with him. I began visiting the college library to replace a previously borrowed book once a week. One week was sufficient for me to make the notes and prepare for four chapters. I gave my blood and sweat in preparing for the exam. After three months, I was confident that I could clear all the 12 subjects in one attempt.

In the evening, I bought one cigarette. I was smoking after three months.

During those three months, I received 4k from my family. The average was 1333rs, and my monthly expenses were 2k per month. (Rent 750 plus mess 1200). I knew I had to do something about this. Selling question papers, as was done last semester, was not an option. That was a plain beginner's luck last time. Besides, I didn't want somebody to complain about me. I wanted to earn money ethically this time.

I had my plan ready after about a week of deliberation. I was good at M3, Mechanics, EDC and ALP. So, I thought of giving personal coaching classes to dumb students. My target was year downed students who failed to go to next year because of M3, Mechanics and ALP. None was there from the CSE branch, so I had to drop the subjects EDC & ALP. I also dropped M3 as mechanics was easier to teach than M3.

After a week's searching, I found dozens of students. I made the list of those names. Out of all those backlogers, I only approached a few students. I wanted to choose students who were willing to clear the subject and give effort. I deliberately left out uncles and super seniors. I knew no teacher in the world could make them pass. I talked with at least ten students, of which six agreed to join me, and with those six students, I started my unofficial private coaching class in Tayde's room. Tayde's room location was good, and the area was calm. Besides, he had a whiteboard in his room. There was no fee for my coaching; if those guys could clear the subject (Mechanics), they would give me the amount they liked. I taught them for two hours every day, one hr in the morning and one hr in the evening. I dedicated weekends for revision. I focused only on four chapters and taught the same things repeatedly. Tayde also assisted me in teaching them and added one new student to our class. Now I had a total of 7 students.

I completed four chapters in two months & three days and then stopped our unofficial coaching class.

We still had one more month for the exam & I could have revised those four chapters in that, but I needed time for myself to revise my 12 subjects.

As I started smoking again and was behind my food bills, I had to borrow 2k again from Aaryan.

Nothing was perfect, but things were falling into place, and I had the guts to stand out firm and face the storm.

When the timetable came for the exam, I was the happiest person. Because I was prepared to face the battle. I knew that I was going to clear all those 12 subjects. I wrote the exam dates on the last page of my register and told myself that I would keep this page with me for many years. So that whenever I look back, I will remember these days, I will remember my preparation, I will remember that I even taught a subject to other backlogers in the same period and I could be a good teacher as well. And this will give me the confidence to achieve bigger things in my life.

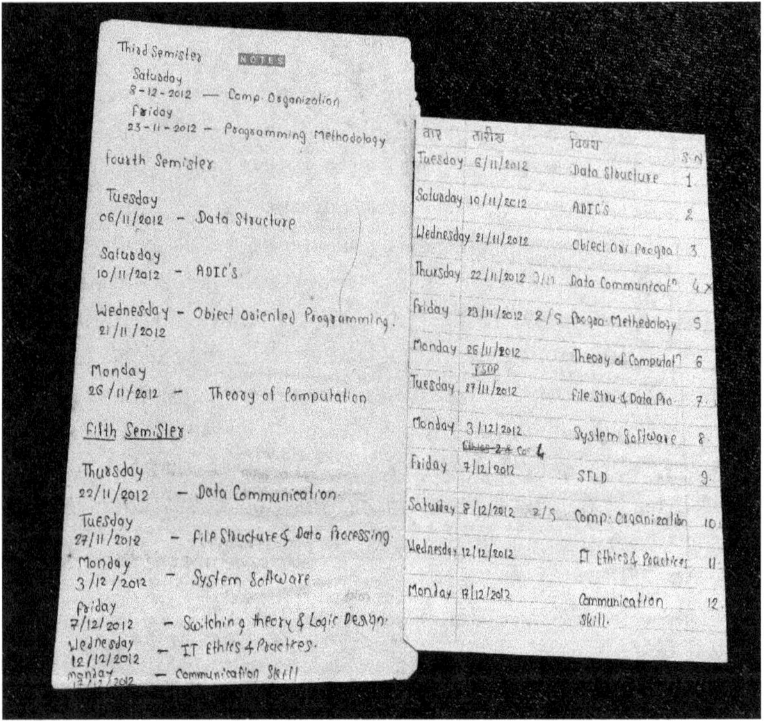

When the result was out, I felt content. The result was as expected. I had cleared all 12 subjects. I had cleared the Theory of computation (TOC) on paper.

I took the mark sheet of the 4th semester, started the splendor and went straight to college.

I stood in front of HOD's cabin. I was waiting for Chopda sir to enter the cabin. When Chopda Sir entered HOD'S cabin to mark his attendance, I went inside and talked with HOD Sir. I showed him the mark sheet and pointed out the Zero internals. I showed that I cleared the subject on paper.

"Congratulations, you cleared the semester. You should focus more on your studies than paying attention to quarrels. You will have a bright career. And I will make sure that nobody gets zero internals without my permission", said HOD Sir.

'Thank You, Sir', I replied, And I left the cabin happily.

After a few days, the result of the first semester was out as well. Out of 7 students, six had cleared Mechanics. They paid 5k, 3k, 3k, 3k, 3k, 2k, and 2k, respectively. I didn't decide any fee from my side. They didn't have to pay anything if they didn't want to. But they all still paid. The guy who couldn't clear the subject also paid I offered 50% of that amount to Tayde as I used his room for teaching, and he also taught a few times instead of me. But he didn't take a single rupee from me.

I paid back my bills and cleared Aaryan's debt. I still had a few thousand left.

On my birthday, all the seven students whom I taught, had booked a reception hall for celebration.

They planned the whole thing so well that I didn't even have the slightest clue about it till the very last moment.

At least 50 people were there for my birthday celebration. I only knew about 10 to 15 of them (my seven students, a few friends from food mess & Tayde). Most of them were seniors and from other branches.

I was wearing a black lower, a black round neck t-shirt and sports shoes as I had never thought someone would do this big setup for my birthday.

There was a large empty ground in front of the hall. When I walked through it, they played a song, 'Shah ka rutba' from a recently released movie Agneepath.

Two girls were at the entrance of the hall holding tilak plates for me.

They had brought a Khanjar for cutting the cake. I cut the cake with that beautiful dagger.

Arrangements of samosa and Jalebi were there for everybody.

"I had goosebumps when you entered with that background song", someone at the party said to me.

I never thought I would get that much respect just because I had taught them a subject.

I knew there will be few things that I will remember the most as I grew older.

Friends like these have taught me the value of friendship.

People will come and go, but those who love you will stay in your heart forever, and the memories never fade.

CHAPTER THIRTY-TWO

Love Inspires

My mother started a tiffin business in 2005, and I distributed those tiffins until I left Buldhana. My departure from Buldhana affected the business, but then my elder sister became a teacher for a well-known coaching institute and started teaching students from grade 5 to 10. That helped the family in a big way. Teaching was in the blood of my family.

She completed her engineering from Savitribai Phule College of Engineering, Buldhana. Her CET score was good, but we didn't have enough money to take admission to the college outside the city. Also, the engineering college in Buldhana was newly opened, and the fee was 20k per year, which was way less than any other engineering college.

Anu di overworked and provided tuitions in two shifts, morning batch from 6 to 9 and evening batch from 5 to 8 along with her college. She couldn't even take leaves during her Semester exams. I am not sure if I or anyone else could have done that.

After her engineering, she joined as a teacher at the same engineering college. The monthly salary was 10k. That was the biggest achievement for our entire family. Until now, nobody had earned 10k per month in my family.

I remember throwing a samosa kachori party in Chinchole Square for the same. Monthly expenses for our entire family were 3000rs to 4000rs, and she could have easily sent me 2000 or more regularly in my engineering years. And she did that for a few months. We were all happy that our good time had begun and there would be no dearth of anything anymore in our life. But fate had different plans. Her college stopped giving salary regularly. They did that with all the teaching staff. They started holding the payments for two months, sometimes 3months and so on. And that was the reason I couldn't get my monthly expenses on time.

But if Anu di wouldn't have been there to shoulder the responsibility of my family, I couldn't have become an engineer. In fact, I couldn't have done anything in my life. She took responsibility for our entire family. She became the sole bread earner, which is why I had the freedom to leave the city and complete my education at a better engineering college.

And I believe she had done all that for her love of family. And now it was my turn to take the responsibility to my shoulder from hers.

I was done with the last semester (8th Sem), and the result was about to come 2 to 3 months later.

When the campus (companies) arrived in the 6th & 7th sem, they didn't allow me to sit as my average percentage was 58%, and the companies needed more than 60%.

I brought back the overall percentage above 60% after the 7th semester's result, but it was too late. No company visited the college in the 8th sem. And I was unemployed, just like the remaining 70% of students in my class. I thought of starting private coaching classes and teaching engineering students, but there was too much competition. Well established and experienced classes were already present in Amravati. And I knew I could only find 10 to 15 students for my class, and that won't suffice. Earlier I just wanted to survive and complete my engineering, which I had accomplished. My current goal was to take the whole responsibility for my family.

Anu di was bearing the whole responsibility of our family. I was so proud that my sister was a professor at an engineering college. Her story of hard work inspired me to do something good in my life.

I had 2 to 3 months in my hand before the result of the 8th Sem would get declared. Most of my classmates had enrolled in CDAC and other coaching classes so that they would get the placement from those classes and would get the job. But I knew my family couldn't afford CDAC or any other classes anymore. So, the next step was to go to Pune or Mumbai in search of a job. But Mumbai was too expensive, so I had to drop that.

Living cost in Pune was less than in Mumbai, but it was definitely more than the cities like Buldhana and Amravati. I knew I had struggled in Amravati because of the lack of money, so it would be very difficult for me to go to Pune without having some initial sum. Furthermore, I didn't have the degree certificate yet as the result of the 8th semester was still pending. I knew I wouldn't get a job without a degree certificate. I could not find any better solution than sitting idle and waiting for 2 to 3 months.

I considered working part-time in Buldhana. I knew the city wouldn't pay me much, but it's better to have something than nothing at all. As I was planning that, our neighbour Aunty came to our house. She came with the job offer. Her brother was a businessman. He had a factory of herbal products, and he was also in the education business. He and his son were selling a career guidance course for the students of 12th std. His surname was Patel. He wanted to talk with me over a call. So, I called him. The discussion was very informal, so I didn't feel any pressure. But I still addressed him as Patel sir instead of Patel uncle to show him proper respect. He promised over the call that my starting salary would be 9k per month, and after three months, he would raise it to 15k. He also promised that I would become a career adviser soon. He told me that I would have to visit schools to teach the career guidance course. My future will be very bright. He promised.

My family was overjoyed that I would be earning 9k per month. They thought that I got settled for life.

"With the Ganpati Ji's blessings, Vijay will become the career adviser. What more can one ask for?" said my mother.

When I was sitting on Veranda bitting my nails in the evening, Anu di came and sat beside me.

"Why don't you tell mother if you don't want to go?", She said.

"Did you see mother's face? How happy she was. And now our family needs money too," I spoke.

Anu Di: Don't try to sound so responsible. I am here to do that.

Me: What do you think? Will I ever do anything good with my life?

Anu Di: Why not? Wait and watch. Someday you will be very successful.

Patel uncle said that if you do your job well, you could be the boss one day.

After hearing that, I smiled.

Anu Di: What happened? Should I have said something else?

I refused by shaking my head.

Me: I'll miss you all.

Anu Di: Yeah, me too.

CHAPTER THIRTY-THREE

Nagar Factory

June 2014 – March 2015

The job was in Sambhaji Nagar (Aurangabad), and I was all set to leave Buldhana once again.

"Do the work diligently and Keep going ahead in life." my mother said as she handed me 3000rs.

I took the bus to Sambhaji Nagar in the morning. I arrived there at 11 AM. I had a Nokia 1600 phone, so I couldn't take advantage of the navigation. I used the traditional way of asking people the direction and went to the office address. I didn't go inside. I just had a look from the outside. There was a small shop named 'Anuradha Associates' on the fourth floor of that large complex. As I found my workplace, I started searching for a room to rent in the nearby area. I searched for rooms until it became dark outside. In the evening, I finalized one room. The room was spacious with good ventilation, and the rent was also less than other rooms. The rent was 3000rs per month. One person was already staying there, so I had to share the room with him, and the rent would be 1500rs for both of us. That's how I met my new roommate Mayur Kanke Patil.

The next day I went to the office at ten o clock. The shutter was wide open and rolled over to the top. And inside was a hall of size 12 by 16. Mr Patel had made two compartments in that hall. A Small one for his personal use and another one for his two workers. There were a total of four computers in the worker's section. His two employees had already occupied two.

Patel Sir took my informal interview in his personal cabin. He asked me basic questions like tell me about yourself and your hobbies.

"I enjoy reading, writing, and mountain climbing", I said.

"What was the last book you read?" He asked.

'Rich Dad Poor Dad', I replied. Then he asked about the book's synopsis.

I defined assets and liabilities. I also provided examples of both.

I told him that his car was a liability, which was a little difficult for Mr Patel to digest.

"You will work under me and Uday (his son)", Mr Patel said.

My job was to call the principals of schools and convince them to purchase the Career guidance program for the entire school. And then Uday will go to those schools to give the coaching.

Mr Patel informed me that I would accompany Uday to those schools to provide coaching in a few months.

Then he talked about the most important part: My salary.

"Since you don't have any work experience, your starting salary would be 6000rs per month, and we will increase it after three months." He stated.

That sentence was a direct contradiction to what he promised over the phone. He had told me that my starting salary would be 9000rs and in three months it will be 15000rs. I knew that nobody would give me 6000rs in Buldhana. It's better to have 6000rs than nothing, so I kept quiet.

My office hours were 9.30 AM to 6 PM. He introduced me to two of his employees from the firm, Monali Mam and Deshpande Sir. Then he left the office. He didn't assign me any tasks. So I sat in my chair and did nothing but look around.

After some time, I started talking with Monali Mam & Deshpande Sir. They opened up earlier than I expected. Monali Mam was in her thirties, and Deshpande Sir was in his forties. Monali mam was a strong independent, unmarried woman. Deshpande Sir had recently bought a new house and was expecting a third child. As the first two were girls, he wanted a boy this time.

Because of the home loan and his wife's pregnancy, he struggled to meet ends. Both of them were very loyal to Patel Sir. You could hardly see such loyalty in the 21st century. Both have been working for Patel Sir for many years. Deshpande Sir asked about my salary, and I told him. Then I asked him his. He and Monali mam both were making 15000 rupees per month. At that moment, I realised that my chances of getting hiked salary of 15000rs per month after just three months were very low.

In the afternoon, Uday came to the office and again took my interview. He was seated in the same chair as his father.

After the interview, He gave me the lines I should use while calling.

The starting was like this, "Hello Sir/Madam, I am calling from Anuradha Associates, an empanelled agency of CBSE...blah blah".

Then he emailed me a couple of pdfs with schools and phone numbers. He instructed me to maintain the responses from the school principals in an excel sheet. And my work started at four o clock in the afternoon.

The next day, when I worked from morning 9.30 to evening 6 PM, I realised how difficult my job really is. Constantly talking on the phone strains your vocal cords. Deshpande Sir advised me to address Uday as 'Uday Sir'. He was 27 years old, and I was 21. I didn't understand the logic behind calling him sir. But I nodded. After that, I started calling him Uday Sir. In a few days, they hired one more guy, he was 30years old, and his name was Parmeshwar. Parmeshwar was a chill guy, and I didn't have to call him Parmeshwar Sir. But he was also told to address Uday as Uday Sir. So, I realised it's not your age that brings "Sir", tagged to your name. It's the money. Parmeshwar had previously worked in call centers and had work experience. He got a salary of 12000rs. Parmeshwar had a completely different personality. He was making half the calls as compared to me & was taking double the salary I took. He never trusted anyone in the office and advised me to do the same. His favourite dialogue was, 'All the bosses are the same. They want people to work under them for long hours and in low wages.'

My joining date to Anuradha Associates was 10th June. I was expecting a salary on 1st July. I calculated that I would get 4000rs for my 20day's work. But I received nothing on 1st July. I thought it was okay as he might have forgotten it and I would get the salary in the same week, but I was wrong. I had paid 1500rs as room rent and 600rs for the food mess. The cost of food in Sambhaji Nagar was less than in Amravati. I was paying 1200rs there, and here it was 600rs. But the room rent was double. In Amravati, I was paying 700 to 750rs, and here I was paying 1500rs. So my monthly expense was almost the same as that of Amravati. My 3000rs which I brought from home, were almost over. So, I had to ask for my salary. I knew Patel Sir was a good person, and he would eventually give me my salary, but I wanted it now.

I got my first salary from 'Anuradha Associates' on 20th August.

Twenty days later than what I had expected.

Perhaps he was following the 'Pay yourself first' rule from Rich Dad Poor Dad.

But I didn't like it.

And I realised this is not the place where I want to work forever.

There was a photograph of 'Mata Saraswati' at the entrance on the wall. Patel Sir told me to place a garland on that every morning.

A fresh garland of Shevanti was coming every day to our office. My task was very simple. Just take that garland from the table and put it over the photo. From tomorrow, I would have to start my day with that.

When the boss (Patel Sir) left, Deshpande sir stood in his place and shook my hand. He congratulated me.

I asked the reason.

"The boss chose you to do the holy work. He must be very happy with your work. You are so lucky", He said.

I just ignored his sentence. There was no end to his stupidity. Parmeshwar had a sly smile on his face as he looked at me. He had got the point.

Deshpande Sir had lost all respect in the eyes of the boss. He used to ask for money from the boss every now and then. He always wanted his salary in advance, and he always wanted 500 or 1000rs in the middle of the month. And that had given boss the liberty to tell him whatever he wanted. For example, the boss used to scold him on why he was having a third kid when he couldn't afford his basic needs. It was the truth, but I wouldn't have scolded someone for that. I mean, it's his personal life. They both were perfect for one another. Nobody was right, and nobody was wrong.

Anuradha, Patel Sir's daughter, visited the office one day. She was friendly with everyone and was down to earth. She was praising Deshpande Sir. Anuradha mentioned how Deshpande Sir handled all of her documentation and government work, such as obtaining the necessary certificates for her since her childhood. "Deshpande Sir, always assisted me ever since I started schooling", She said. Parmeshwar was smiling and trying not to laugh when he heard that. And I understood his point.

One day Deshpande Sir told us one more story from his life. 'I work hard here; sometimes, I even work on Sunday. When the boss goes outstation, I sleep in his house to keep the watch over the house. The last time when the boss went outstation, and I was about to leave from home, my daughter asked me, "Baba, You work the whole day, and now you have to go to work at night as well?" He was laughing while telling the story and everyone laughed. But I didn't find anything funny in that.

After two months, Parmeshwar left the job. He'd gotten another good opportunity somewhere else. The salary was 16000rs. He also invited me to come with him. But I didn't want to ditch Patel Sir that early. Somewhere in my mind, I was still hoping that I would get 15000rs per month once I complete three months here.

Deshpande Sir used to go downstairs and bring tea for the Boss and the important people who came to see him. One day, Boss told Deshpande Sir to get the tea. Deshpande Sir asked me to come with him. We walked down four floors, crossed the highway, and went to the tea shop. Anuradha Associates had an account at this tea stall.

"Tell your Boss to give me the payment for last month. It's still pending', the tea shop owner said.

"Don't worry about your 300rs. They are not going anywhere. Our boss does the transaction of lakhs of rupees daily. He won't run away with your 300rs", Deshpande Sir replied.

I understood the point of that chaiwala. Paying the bills is important but paying on time is more important. But Deshpande sir, didn't seem to get it. I took two chai glasses, one in each hand. Deshpande Sir also took two. And we crossed the highway carefully. This was my first time carrying chai glasses for someone other than my family. The highway was very busy, and the cars were going extremely fast. Sambhaji Nagar had held the record for buying the maximum number of Mercedes and BMWs in one day. The city was full of businessmen and wealthy people. A couple of BMWs and Mercedes had passed us as we attempted to cross the highway. I was looking at the vast difference between those car owners and me. While they were going very fast in their luxury cars, I held two chai cups, one in each hand, and tried to cross the road.

After that day, Deshpande Sir started to take me with him every time to bring the chai.

What kind of an engineer was I, bringing chai for other people? The thought crossed my mind. It was not that I thought this job was small. There is nothing wrong with distributing tea, but it wasn't exactly what I was promised before I joined.

Then the boss began asking me to bring water. That was totally fine. Any elderly person can ask for a glass of water, and I will gladly give it to him. However, his son Uday once asked me for a glass of water. It was a strange feeling to give him the glass of water. I didn't feel bad. I just felt different. But Monali mam felt bad. She complained about him to the boss. And the boss and she (Monali Mam) had a talk. Boss took her side. He said that Uday shouldn't have done it. I didn't indulge myself in that discussion. It was not a big deal for me. I took it as learning how people behave when they have more money than the next person standing.

The following day, Uday arrived in the afternoon, went inside the cabin, sat on his father's chair, and asked me for a glass of water. I handed him the glass of water, and he thanked me. Monali Mams' face turned bright red with anger.

After three months I was expecting that my boss would have a discussion with me about my salary hike as promised. But nothing happened.

My result for the 8th semester was out, and I was officially a computer science engineer. Most of my friends were already in Pune to do different courses. But now, after the last semester's result, those who had not left their hometown were also going to IT cities such as Pune, Mumbai & Bangalore.

My boys, Prakhar, Aadarsh, Sameer & Kishore, were still in Amravati, doing engineering. Sarvesh was doing his engineering in Mumbai; he got dc (discontinued for a year) as well. Aaryan was preparing for GATE. Madhav had enrolled in Veterinary College Udgir to pursue a career as an animal doctor.

My final year classmates were busy searching for IT jobs. Few went to Delhi to prepare for MPSC/UPSC to become IAS/IPS. And I was here in Sambhaji Nagar, working at 6000rs per month and distributing chai and water.

I called my college friend Amar. He was in Pune from June. He gave me the good news that he got selected yesterday by a company called 'Aloha Tech'. The salary was 14000rs, but he was a backend developer, and his work was on C# & .NET. He knew he would get enormous opportunities once he gained some experience. He told me to come to Pune and be his roommate.

"It's not that difficult to get a job in Pune once you start giving interviews. Focus on your communication Skill, aptitude and one technical language", That was his advice.

I was totally confused. I had a couple of options in front of me. Everyone was talking about the job 'Bank PO' at the time (Probationary officer). Working for the government was considered more prestigious than working in the private sector. Furthermore, the starting salary for SBI PO or IBPS PO was 50 to 60k per month, which was way beyond than I ever expected. Even the Bank clerk had a starting salary of 25k, significantly higher than what I was currently earning.

I didn't want to leave my current job and go to Pune unprepared. I decided to try my luck first in the government sector. The next IBPS PO/Clerk exam was in November. And as per the schedule, they were going to announce the result in December. It was the month of August, and I had three months to prepare for the IBPS PO/Clerk exam. I filled out the form.

After my working hours, I went to the city's well-known 'TIME' coaching class. The class duration was four months, and the fees were 7k. I paid a token amount of 2k and confirmed my seat.

I attended my coaching class regularly. The time for the class was 7 PM to 8.30 PM. I used to walk from Anuradha Associates to the coaching class. The distance was 4km.

I used to leave the room at 9.15 in the morning and come back at 9.30 PM. It felt like a 12-hour shift. I realised how difficult it is to work for 12hrs which my elder sister had done for years. I was getting better and better at logic and reasoning questions, and I quickly became the teacher's favourite student in that section. His name was Anand. We used to call him 'Anand Sir'. Most of my classmates in that coaching class were from nearby villages. Their primary goal was to become bank clerks. They were not looking to be a probationary officer. Anand Sir had told in class many times that "Whatever you guys are seeking is not as cool as it seems. Being a clerk is not as prestigious as it appears. The work is boring. You will end up moving files from one location to another. There will be no use of your brain. It's just hard labour. " He was talking from his personal experience. He had worked as a clerk in a private bank. And he didn't like his experience there, so he left the job after a year. And now, he became a teacher temporarily on TIME and was preparing for UPSC. One day in the logic and reasoning class, when I answered all the questions, the whole class was staring at me. I wasn't that bright, but there was no competition for me in the class. Most of my classmates were from Arts background. After the class, Anand Sir approached me and asked, "Why do you want to become a clerk or PO in a bank. You are a computer science engineer. You will get a high-paying job in your field". I listened to him carefully.

His words gave me the direction for my future goals as I believed every word he said.

I continued my routine of going to the office, then to class, and then revising the chapters for an hour before sleeping.

Life had become less than desirous.

On the special occasion of Diwali, the boss gave bonus envelopes to everyone (three of us). This year Diwali was on Thursday (23rd October 2014). In my envelope, I found 1000rs. Deshpande Sir was thrilled with his envelope and praised the boss for his generosity.

I began walking towards my room after office hours. Everybody was lighting crackers, and the coloured rockets were exploding in the cloud.

Celebratory fireworks illuminated the sky.

I like Diwali for a very different reason than other people. For me, it's the loneliest night of the year. I feel different when everybody is happy with their new clothes and firecrackers that I couldn't have. When everyone goes out with their dad for shopping and I couldn't. I have had these memories accumulated over the years, which might sound disheartening, but they are very special to me as they made me independent and strong. On a Diwali night, when the world is filled with Diyas, houses are decorated with lighting and lanterns, and the sky is filled with colourful fireworks, I fill myself with solitude. A Diwali night brings me the feeling of hopelessness, anguish, and despair. And I somehow enjoy it. I enjoy flying solo.

After the festive season when everybody was back to the routine, I was preparing for PO. Exam for IBPS PO and Clerk was scheduled next week. I gave my 100% in the month of October. After my work hours (9 hours) and coaching classes (2hrs), I spent 3 to 4 hours studying. That means I was working 14 to 15hrs a day. After a month of following that routine, I was hoping that I would be able to crack the exam.

The exam date was 2nd November.

It was a sunny Sunday, and I confidently walked into the exam room.

The exam didn't go as well as I was expecting it to go. Perhaps, I was not as prepared as I thought.

I completed five months in 'Anuradha Associates' on November 10th. I was saturated by doing the routine job and attending the coaching class. On November 11th, I initiated the conversation and reminded my boss of his promise to increase my salary to 15000rs. "The salary doesn't go from 6000rs to 15000rs in just 3 or 4 months. But don't worry, I will talk with Uday and he will increase your salary." that was his response.

After three to four days, Uday told me that he had increased my salary to 7500rs.

I was not happy with that raise, but I didn't utter a word.

T.I.M.E coaching class got over in the month of November.

My roommate Mayur had come back from his hometown (from Diwali Holidays). I needed some break from my monotonous life. So, I decided to enjoy every moment I had instead of waiting for something good to come on my way. I was earning 7500rs which was more than enough for my personal expenses.

My roommate had R15. It was the coolest bike around at the time. Roaming around the city every evening became our daily routine. Our evening tea was at Hotel Ram-Bharose. In just a few days, we covered all the best hotels in Sambhaji Nagar. I had to work on Saturday as well, and Mayur had college, so our weekend used to begin on Saturday evening.

Our plan for Sunday was sorted. Wake up at 11 o clock, go to Ram Bharose, and have tea. I used to have a cigarette as well with tea. Mayur was a non-smoker. We always used to have lunch in mess as menu was special on Sunday. And in the evening, dine at a new hotel because the food mess used to be close on Sunday night. After dinner, we used to go to Barkat Tea, which was said to be a 100-year-old tea shop. Some claim it has been there for the past 50 years only. We didn't know the truth, but the chai was good. After that, we used to go to naturals (Natural Ice cream) opp. Akashwani. We sometimes used to go to have a Paan at the famous 'Tara Paan Center'. Both of us were not a fan of eating paan, so we tried different paan flavours a couple of times and then removed that from our Sunday plan. We tried several hotels before deciding that the "Dashmesh Hotel" was the best fit for our taste buds. I had my first sizzler there. I was amazed by seeing the entrance of that dish and how it attracted all the customers eyes on it with its hissing sound.

All the Saturday evenings and Sundays in Sambhaji Nagar were the best weekends in my entire life. Even after doing all this, my monthly expenses were 3500 to 4000 rupees. First time in my life, I was ahead of my bills.

Girl's PG was right next to our building. A girl named Rakul in that PG was very famous for her beauty. Our whole apartment had sent her a friend request on Fb. On one fine Saturday, our conversation turned to girls and then to Rakul. Mayur opened his laptop, cancelled his friend request and sent it again. Then he logged out and asked for my credentials. Mayur had so much faith & confidence in me. He sent her the request from my account as well. After 2 mins, we got the notification. My request got accepted. "She would be your girlfriend in the next few days", Mayur predicted. He insisted on sending her the first Hi. Mayur was more excited than I was. I sent her 'Hi'. I began chatting with her, and within 30 minutes, we were talking on Whatsapp. I took Mayur's iphone, inserted my sim, and started chatting with her as I didn't have a smartphone. After 15, 20 mins, I closed the conversation by sending her a good night. Then I took my sim out and returned his phone. Mayur's excitement had crossed the roof. It was at the level of a kid receiving his first toy. He had already made the plan for both of us.

"Fix a date with her. Take my R15, go to a nice restaurant, and have a candlelight dinner. Then send me the selfie, and I will show it to the whole apartment. So that all the boys should know that she is their Bhabhi."

I didn't want to break his castle of imagination, but I had to. I knew he had gone too far. I had been there. I had done all that in my engineering. Taking Aaryan's bike and wearing Sameer's jeans,

I knew how that ended. It was not me. And I didn't want to make the same mistake again. If I ever go on a date, it would be my bike and my hard-earned money. And right now, I couldn't afford any of that. I knew 6000rs wouldn't be enough if I got into a relationship. There was no place for a girl in my life until I got a good-paying job. I needed to focus on my career first. But I didn't want to explain all this heavy stuff to my close friend Mayur. So, I just told him that I was not interested in her, which was really shocking to him, and it took him days to digest that.

I called Sarvesh and Madhav & told them to come to Sambhaji Nagar. Sarvesh couldn't come due to his exams, but Madhav arrived on Friday night. I took a day off on Saturday. It was my first PTO in the last six months. We started our site seeing on Saturday. We went to Panchakki first, and then we saw Bibi Ka Maqbara. The distance between Panchakki and Bibi ka Maqbara was 1.8 km, and the auto wala was asking 50rs. 50rs was too much for us, so we walked. Then we went on to see Sambhaji Nagar caves. That was 3km further from Bibi ka Maqbara. We asked for the fare. Someone said 200rs; we laughed and started walking. The guy then offered 100rs as his last offer. We declined and kept on walking. 3km and 5km walk was nothing for us. As auto wallas usually tell higher rates to people coming from different cities. But the auto wallas didn't know that they were messing with the wrong people today. We saw the caves, then we ate at one excellent Dhaba on the way and came back walking. We enjoyed every bit of that day, including the time we spent walking. Madhav returned on Monday, and I was back to my boring office life.

On December 7th, there was engagement ceremony of my elder sister Anu di. I did shopping after a very long time. I had saved ten thousand rupees until now (after paying the entire coaching class fees). I spent 3k on my clothing and bought a smartphone for my sister. The model was 'Redmi 1', and it cost 6k. My sister was a professor at an engineering college, but still, she had never used a smartphone. It was a perfect gift for her. On the occasion of her engagement, I gave her that phone. Everybody was so happy at the function. My goal was to take responsibility for the family before her marriage. Anu di's marriage was going to happen in April or May 2015. I still had four to five months. I somehow needed to earn 10k per month to manage expenses for myself and my family. Right now, I was not sending a single penny at home.

After a few days, the result for IBPS PO & Clerk was out. I couldn't crack the written. I didn't have enough time to wait for another IBPS PO/Clerk or SBI PO/Clerk exam. I had also given the exam for the Job 'Aarogya Sevak'. The required education for that job was 12th. And I was an engineer. But still, I couldn't crack that exam. Some say only people with contacts get govt jobs because of corruption. But I was not sure. Maybe I had not prepared well for govt exams.

After work one evening, I went straight to the railway station and sat on a bench in a quiet corner. I wondered what I was really doing. I was an engineer but working as a tele caller in Sambhaji Nagar. It's not that I thought the job was small, but I didn't know how I would go ahead. Only I knew what was going on in my life. I went to a job and worked hard for nine long hours, completed four months of coaching & prepared for the exam every single day no matter how tired I felt, but I couldn't crack the exam. I gave my best, but I was still seeing failures everywhere. I was not getting any opportunity to progress. How long will this go on? Sometimes I even felt like quitting everything and going back to Buldhana. But then I thought about my mother's face. Every night when I returned to my room, I felt like life had beaten me today as well.

Today I was sitting at this quiet bench, but I realised that this is what I had kept thinking for the past few days, no matter where I sat. I spent the entire night at the railway station. I watched trains coming and going. I observed people entering and exiting the compartments. The time flew, and the sun rose in the sky before I could realise it. I stood from that bench and called Amar.

"I will come to Pune soon. Be ready to make some space for one more guy in your room".

I decided to save some money for my voyage to Pune. I planned to leave 'Anuradha Associates' in 2 months.

I planned to travel to Pune on March 1st. I saved three thousand rupees in January. On February 5th, I informed the office that I would be leaving at the end of the month to pursue a job in my field. Patel Sir warned me that getting a job in Pune is not that easy.

"We also want you to earn 25000 per month, but everyone knows how many unemployed engineers are there in Pune", He said. And he was right. But that truth couldn't stop me from going and trying for myself.

Deshpande Sir forewarned me that I was about to make the biggest mistake of my life. According to him, I would never get such a good boss in my entire career. Deshpande Sir also told a story from his life, "I have been working with Patel Sir since 1992 (Or maybe 1996; I don't remember the exact year he told). I had made the same mistake of quitting my job. Then after that, I couldn't find anything outside, so I had to come back. Patel Sir had generously gifted me a new cycle at that time. I still remember that. That was my first cycle" I carefully listened to his story and then continued my daily work.

I told Monali ma'am to inform the boss that I will be leaving Sambhaji Nagar on March 1st and will require my salary on time this month. I expected to get the salary on February 28th, but that didn't happen. March 1st was a holiday (Sunday), so the office was closed.

My birthday was on March 2nd. On the night of March 1st, Mayur and I saw a movie at the Sambhaji Nagar PVR. There was no plan for cake or anything. While watching a movie, I told him that I would love to have a cigarette exactly at 12 o clock.

"You will have it", He promised.

The film ended at 11:45 p.m. Mayur, and I came out and rushed towards bike parking. Mayur drove the bike at 110, 115km per hr. And at 11.58 PM I was in front of a paan thela. He fulfilled his promise. There was a cigarette in my hand at 12 o clock.

The following day, I went to the office to collect my salary. Everybody (Boss, Deshpande Sir, Monali Mam) wished me a happy birthday. The Boss gave me my salary. And I bid goodbye to everyone.

The job at 'Anuradha Associates' had taught me many things. My communication skill improved.

But the best thing that happened to me in the last nine months was I met Mayur. Even in all that chaos and hectic schedule, I had enjoyed my stay in Sambhaji Nagar.

I packed all my belongings in 30 minutes and was ready for the next adventure. Mayur came with me to the travel stop. Before I could get onto the travel bus, he hugged me.

"The only reason my days in Sambhaji Nagar became bearable was you, my friend", I said while bidding a goodbye to Mayur.

CHAPTER THIRTY-FOUR

Darkest Days

March 2015 – June 2015

The news of leaving the job in Sambhaji Nagar made a blast in my house. My mother was not happy at all with that. She had believed Patel Sir's words that I would be a star in that job in a matter of months. In her mind, I hadn't just kicked the job, but I had kicked my bright future. I was in a place where no one wanted to be seen. Even if my decision sounded insane at the time but I knew it was the right decision. I had the guts to follow my heart and intuition. To convince my family that my decision was right, I had to take it to a whole new level.

On March 3, 2015, I arrived in Pune. I had six thousand rs in my pocket, and that was my hard-earned savings from the last two months. I was carrying two dresses and a large number of books which I had accumulated in T.I.M.E coaching and some from my BTech years. The total weight must be between 15 to 20kg. Most of the weight was because of books. When I got off the bus, a couple of auto drivers surrounded me. I wanted to go to S.N.D.T sq. I was 1.5km to 2km away from Shivaji Nagar. I knew I could get the city bus from Shivaji Nagar. Autowalas were asking 300rs for that 1.5km. They knew that I had a lot of luggage and must have thought I couldn't walk with that. I didn't even have a smartphone to use navigation. But still, I picked up the bags and began walking in one direction; after a while, I asked people for directions. My bag had a sharp handle, so holding it was more difficult.

In 30 to 40mins, I reached the Shivaji Nagar CT bus stand. I kept my bags on the ground and looked at my hands. They had turned red and blue. But I was happy that I had saved 300rs.

After another 30mins, I got the city bus, and I reached S.N.D.T stop. I called my friend Amar and told him to come there to receive me. After 20 mins, he reached. In that time, I had tea & cigarette. Amar's room was near S.N.D.T stop. It was a large hall with a total of five people staying there. I was the 6th one in that hall.

I met my classmate Vikram there. Amar, Vikram & I were classmates in engineering.

I didn't have a mattress, and I didn't have a pillow; I just had one bedsheet, and that was it. There was only one bathroom and one toilet for all of us. And the rent was 2000rs for everyone. Earlier they were paying 2400rs, but with me being there it became 2000rs for everyone.

We were all engineers who had come to look for jobs. Three people were doing CDAC, and they were confident that they would have jobs in a few months via the CDAC campus. Only Amar was fortunate enough to have a job. The other two (Vikram and Narayan) were like me, searching for a job on their own.

I gave 2000rs as room rent, and now, I had near about 4000rs left. I knew that I needed to spend that cautiously. The first thing I did was I stopped smoking. That saved me 200rs per month. I knew it was not much as I was not a chain smoker. And I never liked alcohol that much, so I didn't have to worry about spending money on that. Everyone was trying to save money and reduce the cost of living as much as possible. We were all living like misers. It was not that the other guys were poor, but there is an age for boys, and after that, we all feel ashamed to ask for money from our parents. We found a place where people used to get food in 20rs. All the labourers used to eat there. In those labours, we three (Vikram, Narayan & me) became an addition. We used to have lunch there. As Amar used to have lunch in his office cafeteria, he couldn't give us his company. We also found a good place where the cost of a delicious thali was 50rs. And if you want egg curry, then the cost was 60rs. For non-veg thali, the price was 90rs. Vikram, Narayan, Amar & I used to have dinner there.

The day used to start at six o clock and end at 1 AM for everyone. Everyone used to study like crazy. They all had smartphones & laptops apart from me. Narayan was in multiple job-hunting groups and had subscribed to a couple of such channels. As a result, he used to get emails. Vikram and Narayan used to go for off-campus interviews together. Now we three started going together. We always preferred the city bus to go out. It was the cheapest mode of transportation. Narayan was so up to date that he used to get messages every other day for off-campus interviews, and we used to attend that. My saving of 4000 was eroding very fast. Most of it was going for the transport. We used to start our journey (for off-campus) at seven o clock and used to return at night. Many times, we just stood in the line from morning till evening without food, but our number never came.

It was the month of March & April. And the Sun was our enemy. Travelling in the afternoon and walking from place to place was becoming difficult day by day, as the Sun was becoming angrier every passing day.

On 9th April, I was left with just 10rs in my pocket. I borrowed 3k from Aaryan for one last time and decided that I would no longer take money from him. I had already owed him 2500 of petrol from the final year of engineering. So, the total had reached 5500rs. I needed to do cost-cutting. I couldn't do it on travelling; otherwise, how else would I get the job? And it will defeat the purpose of coming to Pune. So, I started having dinner at the same place with the other labourers where we used to have lunch. That was saving me 30rs daily and 900rs per month. The food was not enough for my stomach, but I got used to it in a few days. Vikram & Narayan advised me not to do that and have dinner with them in the 50s. But they didn't know the whole story, and I didn't want to share it with them either.

The borrowed 3k was reduced to 1k in just a few days because of extensive travel for interviews. We all (Vikram, Narayan & I) were getting rejected in every interview. Sometimes we cracked written and got rejected in the face to face interview, but most of the time, we didn't even get the chance due to overcrowding. "Our vacancies are full for now; please visit next time", became the routine dialogue we had to hear.

All of us jobless engineers were accustomed to talking with each other, discussing how we spent the day at night. The days were always silent and filled with struggles. But now, even the nights became quiet.

Vikram was having trouble sleeping one night, so Narayan, Vikram & I went for a walk on the newly built empty road. It was a full moon night.

"Everything on Earth is constantly changing. Nothing lasts forever. Look at this perfect road. It wasn't there when we arrived in Pune," Vikram said.

I thought about it for a while as I looked at the moon and the cleaned road.

"Someday, this night stroll and the dream talks about our future would just be a memory. We will be successful at that time. We won't be job seekers & we will be satisfied with wherever we are". I said.

"Aaahooo", they both said in unison.

We started walking towards the room. Tomorrow was another new day, and we needed some sleep before going back to war again.

One day, Amar referred us for an opening in a company. The interview was scheduled for the three of us. I cracked the written and was waiting for my interview. Vikram & Narayan couldn't clear the written, so they returned to the room. I waited and waited, but nobody was calling me for the interview. Finally, at 7 PM, the receptionist called my name and sent me inside. The interviewer took my interview for 1 hr. I answered 50 to 60% of the questions. So, I was not sure if I would get to the next round or not. I waited for some more time to see the result. And when the result was displayed, I got to know that I got rejected. I started walking towards the C.T. Bus stop with a heavy heart and despair. The nearest bus stop was 1 to 2km away from the company. I was thinking about the interview and was trying to find out what went wrong while walking. I was not keeping a watch on time, and when I reached the bus stop, it was already 11.15 PM. The last bus had already left 15mins back. I had not eaten anything after lunch, and I was hungry. I went to the nearest auto & taxi stand. One auto was getting filled up. I told him my destination, S.N.D.T stop. He told me the fare 60rs. Usually via Bus, it would have cost me 15rs but anyway I was late. And I didn't have the courage to walk 5 miles anymore. Three people were already sitting inside the auto. There was only one last 500rs note in my wallet. I took that last 500rs note out in my hand and asked the auto driver whether he would have the change or not as I didn't want any quarrel when I would reach at S.N.D.T which used to be awfully quiet after 11 o clock. I knew I wouldn't get change for that 500rs note once I arrived there. The auto driver nodded, signalling that he had the change.

As I was about to sit inside the auto, a man grabbed my hand from behind and took that 500rs note from me.

"You are coming with me in my taxi. And the fare will be 500rs which you already gave me. Now tell me where you wanna go?", He said.

The man was 6 feet tall. He was either drunk or high on something else. But he was not normal.

"Give me my 500rs back", I said.

"No. You tell me where you want to go. I will take you there", He said.

"Give me my 500rs back", I said one more time.

There were more than 20 auto drivers and taxi drivers there. They all were seeing the show. It was kind of a live entertainment program for them. Few were laughing.

"Don't you understand the language? I am asking where you want to go?", He shouted.

The situation became tense in seconds.

I put my left hand on his right shoulder to have a proper grip and punched him very hard in the gut.

He vomited the next second.

I twisted his hand & took that 500rs back from his grip, and looked around. Nobody was laughing anymore.

I went back to the auto, sat inside & told the driver to start. He started the auto. Four people were sitting on the backside, including me.

The driver was the 5th one.

The journey was immensely quiet. Nobody uttered a word.

The cold air was touching all of us.

When the auto arrived at the S.N.D.T stop, I got out and took the 500rs note from my wallet. "Uhh. Don't worry about that. You don't have to pay anything", said the auto driver.

I insisted again. But he was refusing to take the money.

"I am just a guy who stayed away from fights and quarrels all my life" I wanted to tell him that, but I couldn't.

I deliberately gave that 500rs to him. He carefully took out crisp notes from the bundle and gave me 440rs back.

At the month-end, I got 3k from my family. That was for shopping as my sister was getting married on 7th May. I knew that was the last amount I was getting from my family for the next couple of months, as after marriage, we won't have anything. I bought a sky-blue shirt at 300rs, bought trousers at 700rs, bought shoes at 250rs & purchased a blue blazer at 1200rs.

My health had deteriorated, and nothing was looking good on my body. My weight had come down from 61 to 50 in just two months. But I was looking forward to the marriage ceremony which was scheduled for 7th May.

On 1st May, there was an off-campus interview for the company 'Vodafone'. The initial package was 4.2L, which was way more than my needs.

I cleared written, GD (Group Discussion), and the first interview. Following that, there was a lunch break.

Around 4 PM, I gave my second interview. That also went well. The result was to be revealed on 4th May.

I needed that job desperately. I knew I would be the happiest person in the world if my name was there on the selected candidate's list. What else one would want if he had the offer letter two days before his sister's marriage. I also wanted to do some show off in front of relatives.

My sister had left the professor's job as she would be relocating to Nashik after marriage. Her job was the backbone of my family, and we all were surviving on that. And that was about to come to an end. It was the need of an hour for me to get the job for the sake of myself and my family.

On the 4th of May, I logged into Gmail from my sister's Redmi 1 phone, which I had bought in Sambhaji Nagar.

I had received a mail from Vodafone. Before opening that mail, I closed my eyes and prayed to God for 5mins. Then with a heavy heart and excitement, I opened the mail.

Hi Vijay,

Thank you for taking time out to interview with us.

After much deliberation internally,we **regret** *to inform you that we will not be able to go ahead with your candidature for the current position.*

However, we would like to associate with you, should any suitable position open up in the near future. You may also touch base with us after 6 months, which is the minimum period before which we can interview you again.

Please   visit   our website..

...

After the word regret, the rest content became a blur to me. I couldn't read it further.

If there was one thing I desperately needed at the time, it was that job.

If God could only have done one good thing in my life, it would have been this job.

But no. He didn't.

I couldn't get it.

The pain of rejection was not bearable.

I attended my sister's wedding with a heavy heart while hearing taunts from relatives. The most common taunt was, "Today's kids don't listen. Every street is filled with jobless engineers, but still they deliberately waste parent's money".

I talked with my father at the function, and he told me to visit his room as he was also in Pune.

After the function, when I came back to Pune, I was broke again. I borrowed 800rs from Vikram and pushed my misery a little bit further. Those 800rs bought me some more time. I was feeling the darkness of the time. I reduced my eating to one time. So, my eating expense came down to 20rs per day. My family was also going through a difficult time in Buldhana. During that period, I received a call from relatives asking for 25k as that was needed to give to the "Ajanta Mangalkaryalay" (Marriage-hall) owner. I wanted to tell them that I don't even have money to eat, so how could I give 25k. But I couldn't.

After my sister's marriage, I knew that relatives wouldn't provide me with any help. So, there was no point in calling any of them and asking for money. I called Monali mam from 'Anuradha Associates' and requested her 3k for a few months. But as per the conversation with her, she didn't have any to give. And in a few days, those 800rs I had borrowed from Vikram were also gone. In my SBI account, I had 98rs left, so I told Amar to transfer me 2 Rs, and then I took out 100rs from the atm. Amar's situation was similar to mine, and he was sending the majority of his salary to his home, so how could I ask for money from him? I called Maddy from Amravati and borrowed 100rs from him.

Then I dialled my elder sister Anu didi's number and asked for 100 rupees. But she advised me to come to Nasik (to her home). She was ready to give me three to four thousand rs but only in person as she was new in the city. I didn't tell her the whole story. I didn't tell her that I was starving. How could I? She was new in the city, recently married. How could I drag my suffering to her new home? "She has already done enough for the family", I told myself.

"I will come to Nasik soon", I assured her and ended the conversation by cutting the call.

I thought of calling Sarvesh and Madhav, but both were still in college, dependent on their father financially. How could I ask them? And what would I say? That I am starving and send me some money? That thought was horrible.

I was in the middle of the ocean and was getting out of breath with every passing minute. And I knew I would drown any moment. But still, I didn't want to tell my condition to anyone. I just wanted to hold on as long as possible.

One day, all three of us received a mail from a startup, and the interview was scheduled for the evening. The office was very near to the S.N.D.T stop. So we all (Vikram, Narayan & I) went there walking. As usual, all of us got rejected. While walking back to the room, Vikram and Narayan wanted to go to a certain place to have dinner. I told them I have some work, so you guys go ahead, and I'll join you later. Little did they know that this was my 2nd day without food. When they took a turn and were not in the view anymore, I started walking towards the room. As the sun began to set, I felt like I was in a strange land, and I had nothing. I was all alone in the worldI was feeling sorry for myself. I had never imagined that my life could take such a dark turn. I had lost faith in myself, and I wanted to cry. I had never wept in front of anyone. But the roads were empty, and I was far from home, so I wept. I wept while looking at the sky because God was unfair. This was the way God had repaid me because I believed in my dreams.

The next morning, I was going out to take a xerox of my resume. This was my third day without food. I had only 3rs which were about to get spent on the xerox. I started to feel dizzy, and each step I took made me feel fainter. I was on the sidewalk of Paud Phata road. On my left was a temple of Dashabhuja Ganpati. I realised I needed to sit, but I just wanted to go inside the temple and sit on the bench instead of sitting on the road. The road was made of interlocking cement tiles. My vision started getting blurry. In a few seconds, everything became completely blurred. And there came the point when it was too late to do anything. I lost my consciousness, and before I knew it, both of my knees hit the ground. That broke one of the tiles, and the broken piece of the tile jumped in the air. Then I collapsed to the ground. I am not sure how long I was sleeping on the road like that, but I felt people walking over me. I overheard someone, probably an elderly lady, "Nowadays, students get addicted to alcohol at such a young age. And see; this is their condition".

"A Sadhu from the Dashabhuja Ganpati temple approached me and took me inside. He gave me a glass of water and whispered, "It's **magical water**". After drinking that, I gathered all my strength again. I thanked the Sadhu, took his blessings, and started walking to my room.

Unfortunately, it was all in my head. For a while, I considered it real as I could not differentiate between dreams and reality. But the reality was ugly. I was still sleeping on that road.

CHAPTER THIRTY-FIVE

Back to the Future

Year 2016

I received a 35% hike after just completing a few months in Deloitte. It was time to move out of the PG. I was living with Akhil & Himanshu. We three moved to a 2bhk flat in a nice society where the rent was 18k, and the maintenance was 3k. I took a master bedroom for myself, and Akhil and Himanshu took another room. So, I paid 9k rent and 1k maintenance. They both were paying 4.5k rent and 1k maintenance. We converted that semi furnished flat into a fully furnished one in just two weeks. We bought all the necessary things like Washing Machine, Refrigerator, ACT internet connection and Gas Cylinder setup. We found the best cook in the area.

Having parties at the flat became a usual thing.

It was time to explore new places, go on vacations, take the bike and get lost in the mountains. And I did exactly that.

Life was not that complicated. I was exploring the places while exploring myself. Maybe I was looking for something.

I can't lie. I did enjoy the company of a few women. Kriti (with long hair till knees) from Pune visited Bangalore, and we spent a week together. Radhika from my current company, Deloitte, wanted to keep it a secret from office colleagues. She had concerns about her image with co-workers. So, we kept it that way until she left the town and got relocated to Delhi. Vaani (a Radhika friend) wanted to enjoy her life before leaving India to do MS abroad. My flat got accustomed to seeing classy girls.

I didn't have a dearth of anything, but one thing was never far from my thoughts, "In this mundane world, how nothing is permanent, nothing lasts".

On one nice evening, while I was sitting with Akhil and Himanshu at Chulha Chowki Da Dhaba and eating the tandoori chicken, I just had this feeling that I couldn't explain or talk with someone. It was just a vague awareness about something. I just thought back on the last year and what I had accomplished. And I realised that I ate non-veg every single day. At least once a day. No matter if it was a Monday or Saturday, I never cared. Ekadashi and Shravan couldn't stop me. I grew up as a vegetarian as my entire family is vegetarian. I was a vegetarian until 12th grade. Although I started eating non-veg in engineering, it was very limited, like once in 6 months, as I couldn't afford it at that time. But now, here in Bangalore, there was nobody to stop me. That strange thought & a sudden sense of self-awareness was killing me from within.

The next day, I visited a couple of shops and saw how they killed those chickens and cut them into pieces. Then I saw Goats getting slaughtered. The shopkeeper could not understand my purpose for being there as I didn't buy anything.

After that day, I never ate non-veg again in my life.

Life is much more than what we make it out to be. There is a time in your life when you feel the need for true love when you feel the need for inner peace when you feel the need for happiness, and that helps you understand life better. Somehow, I was missing all that. I got the company of women, but I never got that irrevocable & unconditional love until now. In my generation, we young people never wanted to get to the point where we know each other so well that we will get bored of each other. The relationships were short, sweet and simple.

Everyone was immersed deeply in sense pleasures and frivolous worldly enjoyment, including myself. But my heart wanted something more than that, something which would last forever.

Sometime after that, I met Nidhi. She was in my office but in another team. She had a beautiful smile and crystal-clear sharp voice. The girl who would change my life forever.

I asked her out one day, and we met after the office.

I could feel the strength of her personality by looking into her eyes.

The more I knew her, the more I wondered how come somebody would be so selfless. In this world of duality and deceit, I had found a naïve girl.

We started spending more time together. Before we could understand, we both were in deep love. I never thought I would meet someone who could understand me without words.

Life becomes much better when you know you have someone who will be there for you no matter what. Someone on whom you can rely.

I had understood one thing, "In the darkest times, things like money could do good but only up to a certain extent. What we truly need is love, hope, and support. That's what we yearn for."

I always wanted someone who would love me unconditionally, not just for my money or the materialistic things I possess. And after spending some time with Nidhi, I realised she was the first woman who had the qualities I was looking for.

My feet were not touching the ground. I was seeing the springs and fountains of love wherever I looked. Her beautiful eyes had stolen my heart, and even upon wanting, I couldn't stop myself from taking a step into the realm of love. I knew we were meant to be together. She was the only thing in my entire life I've never had to think about.

I started roaming with her all over the city and nearby places every weekend.

One Friday evening, as we were strolling beside Ulsoor lake, I told her, "I am not sleeping very well, and even when I am awake, I can't concentrate. I think about you the whole time. There is only one remedy to my illness, which is to make you mine forever. We will get married. And I will make you my wife, but before that, we will have a torrid affair".

The next day (Saturday), I asked her to come away with me.

We saw the magnificent Hogenakkal falls.

The Kaveri River forked into multiple streams and fell through numerous steps, making the sight a mesmerising thing to behold.

We rode a coracle boat from one end of the river to the other.

These were the best days of my life. We talked over the phone all night. We ate whenever we felt like eating. We didn't follow any schedule. We covered all the nearby places in Bangalore.

Nidhi's brother's multiple calls asking where are you? And what are you doing? Couldn't stop us. Office workload couldn't stop us, heavy rains and bad weather couldn't stop us from seeing each other every day. It was our time.

Nidhi was eight months older than me. She belonged to an upper-middle-class family. Her parents had started looking for a groom for her. And to become eligible in the eyes of her family, I knew I had to take some action. I was 23 years old, and my in-hand salary was 34k per month, which was far more than what I needed, but I knew it wouldn't be enough to convince her parents. I planned to make my salary double after every 2years of service. My goal was to buy assets when the salary would reach 50 Lakh per annum. I wanted to become financially independent before the age of 35.

Year	Salary in Lakh per annum
2015	3
2017	6
2019	12
2021	24
2023	48

I had become greedy, I know, but you either become greedy when you are young and then work for it and achieve it, or you stay greedy for the rest of your life. I never wanted to become ultra-rich, but I wanted my financial independence.

I knew people would consider me crazy if I told them this plan right now. Even in 2017, they will laugh. But in 2019, they will start believing a little. In 2021, my plan will look sensible to them, and in 2023 they will treat me like a different person altogether.

People lose control over what's happening in their lives at a certain point, and then they blame fate for everything.

I was not a prodigy, but I always believed in my plans, and I had 100% faith in myself.

For me, everything was possible. I was not afraid to dream and yearn for the things I wanted in my life.

Taking chances against all odds is a rare thing and that's what makes life exciting.

I wanted to have my own house in Bangalore before I turned 30. And I wanted to do it all by myself. The goal was difficult but not impossible.

The simple things in life are the most extraordinary, like having a roof over your head, two times food, good health, and a lovely family; very few understand that.

Making the plan is easy but doing what it takes to achieve it is what separates Men from the Boys.

Being with Nidhi was enough, but only for now. I was ambitious. I wanted her for myself, not for a few days or months but forever.

CHAPTER THIRTY-SIX

A Ray of Hope

Year 2015

When I regained a little bit of consciousness, I realised I was still sleeping on those tiles. No Sadhu was going to come there to rescue me. The entry gate of Dashabhuja Ganpati temple was just 10m further on my left. It's a funny thing that just 10meters seems like 100miles when you don't have enough strength to stand on your legs. The topmost priority in your life should be your health, but you only realise it when you are really sick & can't even open your eyes.

I don't know how much time had passed since the last thought in my mind. I was drip-sleeping.

Nobody was going to come there to help me. Will I not be able to fulfil my dreams? Is this the end? I was asking myself.

"Wo hey mere sapne waha

Apne bhi to nahi hai yaha

O mere bhagwan bata

Kya hai yahi dastur yaha"

"If God is omnipresent, then he must be here lying beside me on the road", I told myself.

I remembered "Bajrangbali" one more time and took a deep breath. Then closed both of my fists and gave all my strength to stand back on my legs.

Finally, I stood up. But my head was still spinning.

Then I went inside the temple, washed my face and drank a lot of water. I felt better.

Maybe it was really the **magical water.**

Just to make sure that I was not hallucinating again & this was not a dream, I touched the walls and that water tap, again and again, to confirm that this was reality.

I took the Darshan in the temple and walked back to my room.

I realised that "God helps you when you want to help yourself". I also understood that if I want to live, I have to leave aside my ego for some time. Nobody can understand my situation unless I tell them. I had borrowed money, but I never told anyone about my actual situation. I never said that I hadn't eaten in 3 days. It was time to change that. Whom do I trust the most? I asked myself. And two names popped up in my head. Sarvesh & Madhav. The next second I called Madhav. I never wanted to share my pain with my best friends, but I didn't have any choice. I told him the story in short and asked him 500rs. He sent me 5k immediately. I had only requested 500, but he sent ten times more. The commendable thing was that he wasn't even earning anything. He sent me the money which his father had sent to him. So, after giving the 2k room rent, I had enough oxygen to sustain myself for a month.

I had to decide whether to think of myself as a poor victim of the system or as an adventurer in search of a better life. "I'm an adventurer, seeking a better life for myself and my family", I told myself.

I intended to be an adventurer like the ones I had admired in movies and books.

That evening, I received a call from Patel Sir in Sambhaji Nagar. He talked with me nicely. He was concerned about my well-being and was interested in knowing how I was doing in Pune. Then he asked whether I could get any job until now, to which I replied, "No, I couldn't".

He told me that his gates were always open for me, and I could come back to Sambhaji Nagar & join 'Anuradha Associates' if I couldn't find anything better in Pune. He gave me the option if I couldn't make it here. I thanked him for that, and the discussion was over.

Maybe he was a good person who was genuinely concerned about my well-being. But somewhere in my mind, I knew that I would become the next Deshpande Sir for his son Uday if I ever returned.

The struggle of living in Pune was unending. As I only had a bedsheet and didn't have any mattress or pillow, I used half of the bed sheet as a mattress and half as a blanket. The other roommates needed the ceiling fan on top speed, so I had to endure that. I always wanted to do everything on my own. But in reality, it was far more difficult to start from scratch.

I called my father the next day and asked for his address. He lived in Chakan, in a small society and a small rented room. This was the first time I saw his actual residence.

I saw him buying vegetables and then cooking for me. We ate together. I asked him if he had an extra blanket. He took one blanket out of his bag after hearing that. So, I discovered that he had an extra blanket. He washed that blanket and put it on the terrace for soaking.

I spent the entire day there. We went to a nearby temple in the evening because he wanted me to see it.

Then we slept on the terrace as it was a better option than sleeping beneath the ceiling fan as it was Summer.

I asked him about his plan to give back the money to the people (from Buldhana) from whom he had taken it. I also got to know that he had taken a 30k loan from a bank in 2003, which was still unpaid. So, with interest that might have been doubled or tripled in all these years.

On my question, he said, "You don't have to worry about my loans. I will pay them back on my own before I die".

I asked him about the bike he had promised me a couple of years back when I was in engineering. I just wanted to know how he was planning to give that if I would have had said yes at that time.

His plan was to take out the money from his PF account.

While looking at the stars, I realised that refusing him and not taking the bike was the best decision I had ever made.

It was still dark when I awoke, and, looking up, I could still see the stars. The terrace is the best place to sleep, I told myself.

Before leaving Chakan, he gave me 2k in my hand. I refused, but he insisted. So, I took that.

I could see in my father's eyes a desire to earn more, be wealthy, and provide everything the family needs, a desire that was still alive despite being buried, over many years, deep under the burden of old age & a mountain of debt.

When I returned to the room, I realised that I was the only one in my family who had the strength to change the fate of my bloodline.

I was not getting selected for the post of an engineer, but that couldn't stop me from doing other jobs. It was time to change the strategy. I wanted to focus on survival.

It's never too late to do the things you need to do. I told myself.

I started giving interviews for 'Call Center'. In most places, I got rejected because I was overqualified for the job. What a dilemma, those who needed engineers were not ready to take me, and I was overqualified for the other jobs I should easily get.

I was coming back to my room after getting rejected by a call center as I was overqualified. I sat on a bus stand. I thought about my first day in Pune. When I decided to move to Pune, I expected to find work within a week. But even after two months, I was still searching for the Job. The direct bus to Buldhana arrived at the bus stop. I looked at the bus for a while. A thought struck my mind. I felt that there was another way to look at this situation. I was actually closer to my dream. The fact that the one week had stretched into two months didn't matter.

After a few days, I got selected by a call centre. It was a night shift job from 7 PM to 4 AM, and my salary was 15k per month. I was happy with the offer.

The next day I went there on time. The manager was a woman in her 30s. She showed me my desk number and left. I sat on that showed chair and started looking at the desk number blankly.

'Hi, are you a new joiner?' a girl asked.

'Yeah. Today is my 1ˢᵗ day', I replied.

She was the girl having a model-like body. She was 5.6 or 5.7 feet tall & was very slim. She had long black hairs which flowed till her knees. She could have been in the advertisement for Shampoo.

'My name is Kriti. What is yours?', She asked.

'I am Vijay', I replied.

'You don't have to worry about the work on your first day. It's usually for the interaction with the team', She spoke.

I don't know if she didn't have any work or if she was done with the work, but she sat at my desk, and we talked for a long time. Then we went to the pantry and had coffee.

She said that she was in the afternoon shift (1 PM to 10 PM).

She told me about lots of places in Pune and asked whether I had visited them or not.

And my answer was No every single time.

She promised me that she would show me every cool place in the city.

We made plans for the upcoming weekend.

I wanted to say No to her plans because this was not exactly the time for me to see the city, but I couldn't.

The time flew, and before I could realise it, it was 10 PM, and she had to leave the office.

While leaving the office, she said, 'I will see you tomorrow. Now you have to make a habit of bearing my company.'

I must admit, she was a desirable woman, and I enjoyed talking with her. I loved her long hair till her knees.

"Kriti, a girl with long hair. I must remember her name", I told myself.

The next day I reached the office on time.

When I entered and sat at my desk, Kriti waved at me, and I smiled back.

After some time, the manager took me to her cabin and told me that I would have to sign the bond for 1year in order to continue my job.

I never intended to work there for one long year. I just wanted it as a side gig. So, I refused immediately. I thanked the manager while shaking her hand and then came out of her cabin.

My bag was there on my desk. I took my bag (which only had a few documents and C++ notes). Only I knew how desperately I needed this current job. And the meaning of having 15k per month in my life. But somewhere in my heart, I knew if I signed that bond, I won't grow for an entire year. If I get caught up with this job security, then I will never move up in life. It was hard but the right thing to do.

Kriti was sitting two desks apart from my desk. She was talking over the call while typing something. I looked at her while putting my backpack on my shoulder. I thought of asking for her mobile number & telling her that I was not going to come here tomorrow. But then I realised she was just a distraction between me and my goal.

I remembered the nights when I slept without food, then I looked at the whole office, looked at Kriti for one more time & left the building.

I was again a jobless engineer. I desperately wanted to start earning before running out of my borrowed money.

There was no going back for me. I knew I couldn't get anything reaching Buldhana apart from pain and disappointments. When you can't go back, the only viable move is to go forward and leave the rest to the almighty.

While eating with the labourers at 20s (Lunch in 20rs), I asked a group, 'Do you guys know if there is any job available?'.

'Do you know how to paint the iron gates?', One of them asked.

'No, I don't. But I can learn', I said.

Well, you can work in construction and lay bricks with us for now. They give 200rs for a day.

I went with those labourers after finishing my meal.

After the entire day of hard work, I got 200rs in the evening.

I worked with those guys for three weeks. I learned how to paint iron gates. First, you have to remove the rust from the iron with sandpaper. That's the hardest thing in painting and takes 60 to 70% of the total time. Then you have to apply primer as a protection against corrosion. If the primer is too thick, you must mix it with thinner. And at last, you can paint the gate.

In three weeks, I earned 4000rs (I took a rest for a day in those three weeks). You can't study or do anything else after that kind of work. Your body will demand rest. I realised that these labourers are the real strugglers. They don't get a half-day on Saturday and Sunday off like govt employees. If they work, they get money at the end of the day, or they don't. They don't know the concept of weekends. They just work and work and work. But the sad part is that they all get drunk every single night. They earn with their blood and sweat, and they spend it on desi Daru, which doesn't even smell good.

Now I knew I had enough money and what to do once it ran out. I could always go with those labourers and earn 200rs in a day.

I never borrowed money from Sarvesh. I kept him as a backup plan. Because tomorrow, even if everything fails, I would still have Sarvesh.

The worst experience of falling on the road taught me the biggest lesson of my life. Always have a contingency plan. My contingency plan was working with the labourers or relying on Sarvesh, but I knew that in time it would change. I will make it as big as my expenditure for the next five years.

The next day I resumed going to interviews. I was still attending 'Call-center' interviews and not the real ones.

One day while I was waiting for my interview for another call centre job, I overheard a conversation between two guys.

'They are only giving 7k per month, and the duty is 12hrs. Our company is far better than them. We shouldn't have come here.'

And those two guys started going out.

My name was announced for the interview, and I knew I needed to go inside.

But I chose to walk towards those two guys.

I talked with them and asked them about their company.

Out of those two guys, one was willing to give me the information, and the other was trying to hide it.

I got to know from one of them that the company name was "VDMission", and they were hiring.

"So, when is the interview? And what they are expecting? I would like to give it a try", I asked.

The other guy (who didn't want to share the info) stopped the 1st one who was about to answer my question & said, 'Why don't you take my number and call. I will tell you the whole process of the interview. Now we need to go'.

I took his number. And then they both left.

After that, I went inside the cabin with my resume to give the interview for the call centre.

I got rejected under one minute as they were not hiring engineers.

In the evening I called on that number. He didn't receive my call. I called three times, but he didn't pick it up, nor did he call back. And that was expected.

But I knew the name of the company. I searched its address from Amar's phone.

I had to change two city buses to reach there.

The office was in Icon Tower on the 4th floor.

Nobody was there in the office as it was a holiday for the office apart from one guy. His name was Badri.

I spoke with him, and he said that the interview would be on this Friday. He gave me the golden advice, "Your communication skill is good. Just work on your keyboard typing skill. Your typing speed should be at least 40 wpm (words per minute)".

And I realised that typing speed was the primary skill they were looking for. The opening was for a back-office job.

I went to the room and asked for the broken keyboard if someone had it. Nobody in our hall had it. I went to all the rooms in our building.

Our building was kind of an unofficial boy's hostel. In one room, I got the non-functioning old keyboard & that's what I really wanted. The keyboard looked like it had fallen into the dust ten years ago.

I only did one thing for the next three days, practising on that keyboard. My roommates thought I had gone mad.

One also said, "Engineers don't need to worry about their typing skills. "But I knew what I was doing.

On Friday, I went to VDmission; they checked my speed. It was 42wpm. I had passed the test. After that, Sudarshan Sir took my interview. He asked me general questions, and I was selected on the spot.

"Your salary would be 12k per month, and 1k would be deducted as PF, leaving you with 11k in hand," he explained.

There was no bond that I had to sign. The day was June 10th. Last year I joined ''Anuradha Associates'' on June 10th, and now exactly one year later, I have joined another job in a different city.

It was a big coincidence. Even my old Man's birthday was on June 10th. Nobody knew how happy I was to take that back-office job. In the United States, they celebrate Juneteenth (June 10th) as slavery ended on that day. My days of being miserable were officially over. So, in a way, it was a freedom day for me as well.

I joined the company & my training started on the same day. They all welcomed me into their world. In just a few days, I made real friends there. Lokesh, Kartik and Sohail in VDmission became one of my best friends.

After my first salary, I went to Buldhana one Saturday. My little sister had got the engineering college Rising Star in Amravati. She was selected via the TFWS scheme, which means the fees per year were just 7k. My engineering fees for one year were 80k. We were all so happy with that news as we didn't have to pay such a big amount every year for my sister. There was no point in staying in Buldhana anymore. I told my friend Kishore to look out for a room near Kathora sq. in Amravati. As Rising Star college was near Kathora sq.

Kishore & Prakhar were in Amravati, still doing their engineering.

Kishore found a two rooms block at rent 3000rs per month near Kathora.

I deposited a gas cylinder at HP godown and took a receipt from them. "You will get the cylinder there in Amravati once you show this receipt", they assured me.

I booked a 3-wheeler tempo for shifting all the stuff from Buldhana to Amravati. First, the driver said 5k, but then he was convinced at 4000rs. I felt weird while leaving Buldhana. My family had lived there for the last 30years, and what all they accumulated? one bed, two mattresses, one almirah, some clothes and a few utensils, that's it. We had a non-working radio and a non-working TV which I threw outside of my rented house. There was no need to carry that stuff. With a heavy heart, we sat in that same tempo and left the city.

When we reached Amravati and saw those two rooms which Kishore had found, I realised that one of the rooms was unusable as it was a storeroom with a tin roof, and another room was very small & congested. But my budget was also small, and the room was in the desired area. Also, Kishore had found it on immediate notice, and I had to go back to Pune the next day. I talked with the owner and told him that another room is not usable & we don't want it. So, reduce the rent as 3k is too expensive for one congested room. But he was a greedy bastard.

"If you vacate that store room, nobody else will come and live there. Either both rooms will get occupied at once, or they will stay vacant", That was his answer. I didn't fight with him because I knew I would not be here tomorrow to fight back. The next day I left for Pune.

11000rs per month was enough to keep my family and me alive, but I knew I couldn't get complacent. I joined a class, 'Profound' which was at Paud phata. It was walkable from my room. The best thing about 'Profound' was it was cheap. As other institutions were giving packages (teaching multiple subjects), the fees were 40k, 50k and so on. 'Profound' was the only class where one could take either a package or individual subjects coaching. I didn't have money to buy packages (coaching for multiple subjects), so I joined the C# class. My primary goal was to receive company calls instead of learning. I paid 1.5k as a token amount and told them I would pay the remaining amount next month. Vikram also joined 'Profound', but he took a package of three subjects. After seeing both of us, Narayan also joined Profound. Again my schedule became very hectic, two hrs class in the morning and then 8hrs job. I remembered my days in Sambhaji Nagar. I had a similar schedule there as well—a nine hours job & two hours tuition.

I had to run to the city bus stop after my morning class. Because if I missed a city bus at 10 a.m., the next one was at 10.45 a.m., and I'd have to wait 45 minutes doing nothing. I had to change two buses to get to the office. The journey to reach the office was itself tiring. But once I got there, I had to work for the next 8 hours. And I had to repeat all that every single day.

I made great friends in 'VDmission'. They did all my work whenever I couldn't make it to the office because of the interviews.

Four people used to distribute my work among themselves and finish it in no time. I knew I could never repay for their kindness. With each interview, I was only getting disappointments as I was getting rejected. But with each interview, I always learned something new. Off-campus interviews are not that easy. Fifty thousand students show up for the interview, and it's very difficult to get a job in that competition. But that couldn't dampen my spirit. I continued giving interviews. Vikram, Narayan and I were going out together like warriors (for interviews), and we were losing every single fight. But we were getting stronger with each battle.

"Do you think we will ever get selected?" Narayan asked on one lost evening.

"Yeah, we all will get selected. A bright shining future is waiting for us". I said, and we all laughed.

Sunday became my favourite day of the week because there was no office or class on that day. If I could work in IT, then even Saturday would be off. After hearing the work-life balance and culture in IT companies from Amar's mouth (who was the only person in the room having an IT Job), We all left the thought of working for the government or becoming SBI PO entirely. What a peaceful life that would be to work for five days a week & then take double or triple the salary than that of govt employees.

On one Saturday, when I came back to the room with my tired body, Vikram and Narayan told me about an email. They both were very excited. "Tomorrow, we have an interview for Deloitte at 9 AM. We must wake up at six o clock and reach there by 8 AM", said Narayan. I didn't understand why they were so excited. We had given 40 plus interviews until now. There was nothing new. I was exhausted, so I didn't pay much attention to what they were trying to tell me and slept early.

The following morning was Sunday, the best day of the week. On Sundays, I used to sleep until 11 a.m. Vikram, Narayan and Amar woke up at six o clock, got ready until 7, and left for the interview. And I was sleeping. They asked me to come, but I told them to go ahead. Suddenly at nine o clock, I woke up with a feeling of guilt that I didn't go with them.

Then I called Amar and asked, 'You already have a job, then why did you join Vikram and Narayan?'.

'It's Deloitte. Not some random company. It's one of the Big four. If I get placed here, I will leave my current job', He replied.

I didn't understand what the Big four was. But I didn't want to waste more time. I was convinced that I should have been there with my guys.

"What's going on over there? Are any of you finished with the first round or something?" I inquired.

"No. We're still standing in the line. A large crowd has gathered here. At least 200 students are ahead of us. You can still come here and join us", said Amar.

I cut the call the next second and rushed to get ready. Normally, I take 15 to 20 mins to bathe, but that day I just turned two chilled buckets on my head, and I was done in five seconds. I wore my formal, which was the only formal dress I had, and ran towards the city bus stand. As I was 200 meters away from a bus stop, a bus came. Before I could reach there, the bus started running. I knew I needed to take that bus. I increased my speed and tried catching that running bus. The bus was filled with college students. They all started cheering me up while I was running behind the bus. I caught that bus in the next 30 seconds. The whole bus was clapping when I entered inside.

At 10.30 a.m., I arrived at my destination. I called Amar; he waved his hands. He was far ahead in the line. I went there directly and stood behind him. Then Amar told me the meaning of the big four and explained how good the company really is.

Our first round was written. After 20mins, they declared the result. Amar, Vikram & I cleared the written, but Narayan couldn't. The next round was GD (Group discussion). Again, they displayed the result for that in the next 20mins. Vikram and I cleared GD, but Amar couldn't. Amar went to his office and gave us best wishes for further rounds. After 30 minutes, they told us that the next three rounds would happen in Mumbai, and selected students (who cleared GD) will get notified over email one day before the scheduled interview. So, keep an eye on your emails. I told Vikram that checking emails and notifying me would be his department as I didn't have a smartphone or laptop. After a few days, when I was in the office doing my back-office work, I got a call from Vikram. "I got the email from Deloitte. My face-to-face interview is scheduled for tomorrow at 9.30 AM. Just check yours; you must have received it as well. We will go together", He said.

I logged in to my Gmail account and checked for the mail. But I found none. I checked again and again, but I didn't find any email from the company. I left the office and rushed to the room. I again logged in to my Gmail from Vikram's mobile and checked. But there was no mail from Deloitte. They had created ids of students for tomorrow's interview. I knew they wouldn't allow me on office premises without the legit ID. How could they miss my name? Because my name was there in the list of students who had cleared GD.

My mind was saying, "Don't worry, you'll get your email another day. They must be conducting interviews in batches. A Few students tomorrow and the rest on a later date".

But my gut feeling was saying something else. I must confirm with Profound once, I told myself. I took the receipt of the fully paid fees for the C# class to prove to them that I am a student in profound. It was the closing time, so I ran towards 'Profound Classes'.

Only one person was sitting there who was about to close everything. Before I could ask anything, he said, "Please come tomorrow. We are closed for the day".

But I ignored his sentence and explained to him that it was very urgent and I couldn't wait until tomorrow. I told him the whole story in short. I also showed him the payment receipt.

After that, he opened his laptop and checked my name. It was a typing mistake, and they had missed my name. After confirming that, he sent the mail to Deloitte and told me to go to Mumbai.

"By the time you reach there, your id will get created", He assured.

Then I walked towards the room happily. I was glad that I came here; otherwise, I would have missed the opportunity to give the interview.

I went to the room and found my formal blue shirt and black pant. It was in bad condition. I washed it. Vikram warned me that it wouldn't dry as we had to leave in a few hours. But I still washed it. It's better to wear wet clothes than dirty ones.

We took the last City bus and reached Pune railway station at 11.30 PM. We took the general train ticket and caught the train in the middle of the night. We were lucky that half of the compartments were empty. I took a window seat, and when the train started running, I held my formal (that wet blue shirt and black pant) and kept them floating outside the window. My clothes dried in 1 hour. After that, I revised Core Java concepts.

At 5 p.m., we arrived at Kalyan Junction. We cleaned ourselves at the railway station. But we didn't want to wear our formals because we knew they would get dirty before reaching the office premises as we both knew about Mumbai locals and the crowd.

We took the central line local and reached Kanjumarg. We then asked for directions and walked towards Tagore Nagar Junction.

Now we had to take the city bus and go to Hiranandani. But before we could do that, we needed to wear our formals. But there was no place to change. We should have changed our clothes at the railway station itself, Vikram said.

I saw a 'Panpoi' at one corner, which had a wooden compound on three sides. I went there and changed my clothes. I was laughing while changing the clothes there. It was a very strange experience to change the clothes like that at the corner of a busy road. Vikram followed me and wore his formals as well. Now we were ready for the interview.

"If I get selected today in Deloitte, I will write a novel. I will add all my writings from my personal diary there, and I will also add today's journey", I said.

"Don't change my name in the novel. I like my name", said Vikram.

We were pleasantly surprised to see the buildings and the posh area when we arrived.

"This is our company. We have to come here daily from now on", I said mischievously, and we both laughed.

They took three more rounds, two technical and one HR.

I went until the last round (HR round).

"One last question, what will you do if we don't hire you?" HR asked.

"I will keep giving the interviews, and I will learn from each of them. I will rectify my mistakes, and the day will come soon when I get selected by some company". I told him the truth.

After that, HR shook my hand, and the interview was over. At that moment, I realised that I got selected. Vikram didn't go till the last round, so it was evident that he couldn't make it. We both boarded the train back to Pune just in time before the train started.

The feeling that I was having while looking out from the window, I couldn't explain that in words.

After a week, I got the call from Deloitte that I was selected, and I would get the offer letter next week. It was big news, and I was happy, but I didn't get excited or overjoyed somehow. I didn't talk about it to anyone, not even at my house. I was waiting for the offer letter. I remembered the experience of Vodafone when I had told the news to everyone, and in the end, we were all met with disappointment. This time I didn't want to take any risks. Although the scenario was completely different this time as I had officially received the call from the company. But I still waited for one more week.

Finally, I received the offer letter. The package was 3.39L per annum. And my joining date was 7th September 2015.

Then I told everyone about the news.

First September was my last day at VDmission. My colleagues gave me a watch as a gift. They all were very close to my heart as they were true friends. For me, It was not just a watch but a symbol of friendship.

I still have that watch today, and I wear it sometimes.

On 2nd September, I planned to leave Pune. I packed the same stuff again, a couple of books, one plate, one spoon, one glass, two dresses, and a black blanket which my dad had given me. All the roommates came until the S.N.D.T bus stop to bid me farewell. In a few minutes, an AC bus arrived at the stop. I had never seen an AC city bus during my six-month stay in Pune. Either I was too busy with my work or too ignorant not to see it. Perhaps it was just time that was changing for me.

I reached Amravati after the whole night of travel. My mother was really happy to see me. When I entered the house, I knew it was time to change it. Finally, I was able to pay a little higher for house rent. After two days of house hunting, I found a perfect two-bedroom home for rent in the same area. The rent for that house was 5k per month. I told the house owner that I would be shifting tonight.

When I reached home, the owner of the current house (congested room with 3k rent) was standing at the gate. He talked nicely and invited me for tea which I politely declined. Then he came down to the actual point and said, "You have to sign a one year bond so that you won't vacate any random day. Every owner takes such bonds from the tenant in this area". I couldn't control laughing after hearing that.

"Forget about the bond. I am vacating your place tonight", I said firmly.

That sentence was shocking for him. His face was worth seeing.

I called Kishore to help me with relocating, and in no time, my family shifted to a good place.

I enjoyed my three days with the family. I planned to leave on 6th Sept so that I could attend my first day of office on 7th Sept.

I bought a white shirt for my first day in the office.

Deloitte had booked a 5-star hotel for 15days as accommodation for me. I went to a cybercafé and searched for trains. I finalised one train, which was starting at 4 PM from Amravati (Badnera Junction) and was reaching Bangalore (Yesvantpur Junction) at 8 PM. Trains usually get delayed, so I knew I would reach there at 11 or 12 PM. This was my first time travelling outside Maharashtra. "The state would be new, the city would be new & even the local language would be new for me", I told myself.

I had 1700rs left with me, and I needed to survive on that until 30th Sept. Then I will have my salary. I knew I would face difficulty getting a cheap auto or taxi as I would reach Bangalore at midnight. I checked the fare from the railway station to the hotel online, and it was showing 700 to 900rs. Booking a Cab was the safe option for a first timer in the new city. But I didn't have a smartphone to do that. My Jijaji gave me the phone number to book the cabs for Ola and Uber. "You don't need an app; just call on one of those numbers, and a cab will get booked", He assured.

On 6th Sept, I tried to book a tatkal ticket to Bangalore. But they got sold out before I could book. So, I went to Amravati railway station and bought a waiting ticket in sleeper class. My bag from

Pune was all packed and ready.

I took the same stuff and started my journey to Bangalore. The train started on time at 4 PM from Badnera junction; The train took 31hrs to reach Yesvantpur junction. The journey was hectic because I didn't have a confirmed seat, and the train was full. But little did I know that this was my last hectic journey, and I would fly from now onwards.

When I reached Yesvantpur junction, I called those numbers to book the cab. And the guy from the call centre informed me that they stopped the process of booking via call two years ago. Now it can be done only via the app.

I called Sarvesh (my best friend, my contingency plan) and told him to book a cab for me. And he did it in the next 2 minutes. The cab driver called me and said he was in front of Hotel Kamat. Before I could pick up my bag, it started raining heavily. There were several gates and small outlets, and I was not able to locate hotel Kamat. I wish I had a smartphone and Google Maps.

I asked two people for direction, and their suggestions were contradictory. I realised one or both of them were lying. So, I asked multiple people for the same thing. Out of almost ten people, 4 to 5 people told the same direction, and I realised that's the right one. The cab driver called me one more time and said, "Sir, we don't wait more than 20 minutes. It's already 20minutes". I realised I didn't have much time to wait for the rain to stop. So, I started heading in the told direction. After three minutes-walk, the buckle of my suitcase broke. It was the new suitcase I bought for 400rs. Now I understood why its cost was 400rs. Suddenly I heard the tone from my Nokia 1600. It was the last heartbeat shout from the phone as it got switched off due to the low battery. I had charged it on the train, but my battery had issues.

I took a deep breath and then held the suitcase on my head and started walking in that heavy rain. With each step, the rain started getting angrier and more intense. And I was just laughing. The people who were standing at the corner and saving themselves from the rain were gazing at me with a strange look. I am sure I was looking like a crazy guy to them.

Finally, I reached the cab.

'Sir, I have been waiting for you for 30mins', the guy said.

And I thanked him for that.

'How long will it take to reach the destination?' I asked.

'Sir, it's 30 kilometres, so it'll take 1 to 1.5 hours depending on traffic,' he replied.

'Would you like to hear a story then, as we have lots of time' I asked.

'I would love that, Sir', He replied.

I told him my story about the time I spent in Pune. The story ended when I sat inside the cab at Yesvantpur railway station. The driver had tears in his eyes while listening to the story.

"Sir, your story touched the deepest part of my heart", He said.

When we reached in front of the Hotel, he gave me his card and told me to call anytime. Then I asked about the fare. He checked on his mobile and told. 'Sir, it's 780rs, but it's already paid. Must be paid by your friend who booked the cab'.

I wanted to confirm with Sarvesh, but my mobile was switched off.

'Are you sure it is paid? Because I had only told him to make the booking. I didn't tell him to pay.' I asked again.

'Yes, Sir, I am sure. Why would I let my own loss happen?'

After hearing that, I took my broken bag out of the trunk, shook his hand and went inside the hotel.

The hotel room was very lavish. It was on the 7th floor. The bed was too much comfortable. As I got used to sleeping on just a half bedsheet, I felt the difference to greater intensity.

The next day I awoke before the dawn. The city was still sleeping. I took a shower and then wore my new white shirt. The breakfast was ready downstairs—one of the benefits of being in a 5-star hotel. I took a lemon tea in a crystal glass. Then I sat on the balcony of my 7th-floor room smoking a cigarette. I smoked in silence, thinking of nothing, and listened to the sound of the wind that brought the freshness of the morning. It was a morning that would last forever in my memory.

The journey became really simple after that. Everything fell in its place. On my first month's salary, I cleared all the debts I had taken from my friends, which was a total of 10500rs (5000rs from Madhav, 5500rs from Aaryan). I had already paid Vikram's 800rs and Maddy's 100rs from my VDmission's salary.

I cleared the entire family debt in just a few months. The mountain of debt was finally conquered.

I pursued my hobby of mountain climbing and writing.

On one such morning, when I was sitting at the top of Savandurga mountain, which is considered to be among the largest monolith hills in Asia, I realised my whole journey in life was like climbing the mountain. I thought I was alone all the time while climbing it, but in reality, I was never alone. The divine was always with me. I couldn't have done anything in my entire life if I hadn't had such good friends. It was he who came in the image of my friends to be there with me at each step, to give me his hand to hold on to.

It was such an interesting thing that I discovered over time that what I thought was my effort was also not possible without his grace.

Even my efforts were his grace.

...To be continued.